TOOTHPASTE & PEANUT BUTTER

BY TERRY MOORE

ILLUSTRATED BY SCOTT JACKSON

hancock
house

ISBN 0-88839-207-9
Copyright ©1987 Terry Moore

Fourth Printing 1988
Printed in Canada

Cataloging in Publication Data

Moore, Terry, 1936-
    Toothpaste and Peanut Butter
    A How-to Collection of Household Hints
    Includes Index
    ISBN 0-88839-207-9

    1. Home economics - Miscellanea.
    2. Do-it-yourself work - Miscellanea.
    I. Title.

TX158.M65 1987   648   C87-091517-7

Designed and Edited by Herb Bryce
Typeset in Times Roman on AM Varityper by Diane Brown
Pasteup by Lisa Brown
Cover and Illustrations by Scott Jackson

Published simultaneously in Canada and the United States by

HANCOCK HOUSE PUBLISHERS LTD.
19313 Zero Ave., Surrey, B.C. V3S 5J9

HANCOCK HOUSE PUBLISHERS
1431 Harrison Ave., Blaine, WA 98230

TOOTHPASTE & PEANUT BUTTER

BY TERRY MOORE

hancock
house

ILLUSTRATED BY
SCOTT JACKSON

This book is dedicated to my listeners, without whose questions and suggestions it would not have been possible.

Acknowledgments

I would like to thank my wife, Ramona, for her tolerance and understanding. Not to mention the constant "devotion" from Ramona and my daughters, Kathleen, Lisa, and Joanne, and my son, Patrick (the chef), without which this book would not have become a reality. Peace reigns once more in the household. How sweet it is!

A special thank you goes to my mother, Hilda Brown of Victoria, B.C., for teaching me basic self-reliance at an early age.

My thanks also go to Dr. Brent Skura, of the Department of Food Science at the University of British Columbia, for his assistance in the preparation of the nutritional comments in this book.

Thanks as well to Nigel Malkin of Malkin Cleaners, and to Dan Logan of Look Carpet Cleaning, for authenticating the stain-removal information.

This book could not have been completed without the assistance of Robert Scheer, the only man I know who can type as fast as I can talk.

Contents

Foreword

When I first met Terence Patrick Moore, he appeared out of the private washroom adjacent to my office. The washroom had an escape door to the side of the building, and we used it to bring people in and out for discreet meetings. Terry was employed by a competitive radio station at the time.

I liked him right away. We made a deal for him to join CKNW in Vancouver, and he promptly exited the same way he had arrived, with no one the wiser.

That was almost a decade ago, and I've since come to know Terry very well. He's a warm, caring, fun-loving, and generous man. In my twenty-five years of broadcasting, I've never worked with anyone who was more willing to perform whatever function he was asked, or who performed it so well. In an industry with more than its share of over-inflated egos, his attitude and spirit of cooperation are rare.

Terry is best described as a "fun" person; the kind that most people like to be with. He's an accomplished scuba diver, and for a couple of years he and I played on the CKNW hockey team. Terry was always the biggest player on the ice. No wonder. He always stuffed his uniform so full of foam rubber that if he ever fell down he'd have bounced right back up again! (This is probably a great household hint for parents who have children playing hockey.) The team enjoyed Terry, and he'd have been one of our better players except for a slight problem: he could only turn left!

Terry, amongst his other talents, can count himself the perfect homemaker. He's a fabulous cook, and really prides himself on his knowledge of the subjects contained in this book. And so he should. When Terry does his household hints program on radio, the phone lines are jammed. And why not? He's the best!

Terry was born in Winnipeg, Manitoba. Besides being an accomplished Canadian broadcaster, he is also active as a television and motion picture actor. One of his most memorable screen roles was the cigar-chomping father of the cousin in the award-winning motion picture, "My American Cousin." He's also a founding member of the Edmonton, Alberta, opera company; he posesses an outstanding voice. Terry studied singing and acting in New York City, where he also hosted one of the highest rated New York radio programs before his return to Canada in 1970. Terry and his wife, Ramona Beauchamp, now reside in Vancouver.

J. E. (Ted) Smith,
President and Chief Executive Officer,
Westcom Radio Group Ltd.

Preface

My first open-line Household Hints broadcast was a sheer accident. I was working in Calgary doing a 6:00 to 9:00 A.M. music show. My segment was followed by "Problem Corner," which another man hosted from 9:00 to 10:00 A.M. Until one day when he called in sick. At the last minute, the program director asked me to fill in and host "Problem Corner."

Ever since I was a teenager, I had been pretty self-reliant. I had a lot of responsibilities around my home, including doing chores like cleaning, washing, ironing, and even some cooking. I grew up, married, became a father, and then a single parent. So I was very familiar with the day-to-day household situations which the listeners of "Problem Corner" would phone in and talk about on the radio. Much more familiar than the show's regular host, whose tips were, more often than not, gleaned from a large book which he all too frequently had to leaf through for answers.

Because of my greater familiarity with cooking,

cleaning, etc., the show went faster and became more fun with me behind the microphone. More and more calls came in to the radio station's switchboard. After the third day of filling in on a temporary basis, I was asked to take over the assignment of hosting "Problem Corner" on a regular basis.

Since then, I have worked at several radio stations, hosting numerous open-line programs. But in all my years of broadcasting, no other topic has consistently been as popular as Household Hints. In the middle of a hot political debate, someone will phone in and ask, out of the blue, "When are you going to do another hour of Household Hints?"

My listeners have asked literally thousands of fascinating questions over the years. And other listeners have provided countless amazing answers. But this book of household hints is also based on interviews I have conducted with experts from myriad walks of life. Some of the finest chefs from North America and Europe have contributed some kitchen secrets. Professional dry cleaners and representatives from corporations which manufacture household cleaning products have told me tips on soil and stain removal. Doctors of dermatology and representatives from the personal care industry have given me insights on skin care.

I have spoken with clothing manufacturers, chemists, dietitians, appliance experts, spice experts, and thousands of men and women whose knowledge has gone into the making of this book.

In addition, my Hollywood "Personality Profile" interviews have shown me that you and I are not the only people who encounter clogged drains and stained carpets. Some of the most famous stars you can imagine are down-to-earth human beings. They pack lunches in brown paper bags. They have problems with their kids and their houses, just like anyone else.

This book, then, is for everyone.

Introduction

One day at the office, I was startled to get a phone call from a very irate man. It was a good thing I wasn't on the air at the time. He was ready to throttle me. He threatened to sue me. He chewed me out from one side to the other for advice he claims I had given his wife the day before.

I remembered her call. She had phoned for advice on how to clean her large sheepskin rug. It was quite valuable, but over the years it had grown dingy with accumulated grease and dirt.

I advised her to sprinkle the rug with a dry cleaner such as corn meal or cornstarch. She said she didn't have them. I told her she could substitute oatmeal then.

Sprinkle the rug with oatmeal, which will absorb the grease and dirt from the fibers. Start at one end, and brush the oatmeal right through to the other, combing it carefully. Finally, vacuum up all the dirty oatmeal. That was the advice I gave.

"The rug is a mess," her husband shouted. "It's all

matted and caked with lumps of sticky oatmeal."

You see, his wife had used cooked oatmeal!

The moral of this story is the value of common sense. Most advice should be taken with a grain or two of salt. In the case of the oatmeal story, take it with a quarter teaspoon of salt, two tablespoons of brown sugar and half a cup of milk.

The best way to solve any household problem starts with one important first step. Stop and think before you act. Never panic. Unless something is on fire, there is no need to rush.

Read labels thoroughly, so you understand which procedures the manufacturer recommends. Following the instructions properly and applying common sense will save you hundreds, possibly thousands of dollars over the years.

Most importantly, it will reduce your stress and aggravation considerably. And that's something money can't buy.

Out Damned Spot

"Go ahead, line one."
It was a female voice phoning in. "My kids just had a ketchup war. And I lost."

She described a scene which had started peacefully enough. A Sunday morning family breakfast. But just as the scrambled eggs were nearly eaten, her 3-year-old flicked a spoonful of ketchup onto the 5-year-old. His brother retaliated. Soon the 7-year-old was also in on the fray. When the battle subsided, ketchup and scrambled eggs were all over the kids, their clothes, and the kitchen.

It was now Monday morning and she was phoning in to complain that, even though she had laundered their clothes, they still had ketchup stains. "How can I get them out?" she asked.

I could only give her the bad news. It was too late. The problem was, she panicked. She didn't stop and think. It would have been better if she had done nothing but let the stains dry. The ketchup would only

have lost moisture. But by putting the clothes into the washing machine without pre-treating them, and by then putting the stained clothes into the dryer, she had set those stains permanently.

Natural fabrics such as cotton are highly susceptible to stains. The acids found in fruits and juices and tomato ketchup will work as dyes. Heat will permanently lock them into the fibers.

But cotton, linen, and even some wool fabrics can often be cleaned with the most common substance in the world. Water. H_2O.

Since three-fifths of the world is covered in water, and 98 percent of our bodies are made of water, it only makes sense that most food products are made up largely of water. Ordinary tap water, therefore, is our first line of defense in removing stains left by food products.

You will read in this chapter solutions for removing some of the most common household stains with inexpensive products found in the cupboards of most average homes.

These solutions are not the only ones available. On the contrary. We are fortunate today to have available in our supermarkets and corner stores some of the finest household cleaning products we've ever seen. Having been involved in household hints for over 25 years, I have seen that, in almost every instance, the claims which manufacturers make about their cleaning products are true. When problems arise, more often than not they are caused by failure to read the label properly or by not following the manufacturer's instructions.

It would be very easy for me to recommend that you go out and buy bottles or spray cans of ready-made commercial solutions. But that is not the point of this book; rather, it will give you the least expensive ways to take care of household emergencies, using commonly found ingredients, should your bottle of commercial cleaner run dry.

Besides the items you probably already have in your cupboard, you will need two further things to solve most of your cleaning problems. Elbow grease and common sense.

It is interesting to note that many of the commercial stain-removal products available today share a common ingredient. They may be different in color, they may be different in smell, and they may come in different packaging. But they are based around the world's greatest stain remover, water. They also contain chemicals that are designed, when combined with water, to make the water super soft; to reduce surface tension, and to allow the water to get into the fibers and work out the particles of stain. But you do not have to concern yourself with that now. What is important for you to remember is the strength and value of water alone to remove water-soluble stains.

Just about any spillable beverage is water-soluble. Fruit juices and vegetable juices, all fermented and distilled alcoholic beverages, coffee, tea, and milk are water-soluble. Use water to remove the stains they cause.

Start with cold water. Hot water can set some stains.

Vegetable stains, whether from raw or cooked vegetables, dissolve in water. So do those from fruits—citrus, grapes, apples, pomegranates, kiwi—regardless of what the fruit may be, its base is water. Where the stain gets tough is with the natural coloring agent that may also be in it. But even that color is water based, and it can be removed with more water, the addition of extra elbow grease, or a man-made agent to make the water work harder.

Club soda makes a marvelous stain remover. The sodium bicarbonate in it helps soften the water and increase its cleaning power. If you clean stains with commercially available club soda, watch out for sugar. Some brands of club soda contain sugar, and they should be avoided. Besides, you don't have to spend the money. You can make your own soda water by adding a teaspoonful of baking soda to a quart of water. Then stir until thoroughly dissolved. Keep some of this solution in a jar so it will be handy for use in removing such stubborn stains as tomato-based sauces, skim milk, pineapple juice, and even red wine. The more stubborn water-based stains will come out easier with the help of soaps or detergents. Blueberries, strawberries, grass stains, ketchup, peas, coffee, and stains of this nature need soaps or detergents to make the water work more efficiently. Heating the water to temperatures ranging from lukewarm to boiling hot, is sometimes necessary.

Some fruit stains, such as from raspberries, are especially difficult to remove because of their high acid content, along with their color. Fresh tomatoes or tomato juice present the same problem.

In the case of the listener with the ketchup-war stains on her children's clothes, here is the basic procedure she should have followed to remove the tomato-based stains.

Isolate the stain to prevent it from spreading. Stretch the stained garment taut, centering the stained area over a large receptacle such as a mixing bowl. Rinse the stain thoroughly with cold tap water to remove the pulp and larger-sized solid matter. Gradually increase the temperature of the tap water, while working the stain with your fingers. Then add a small amount of liquid dishwashing detergent, and work it into a lather. Keep washing and rinsing and re-lathering with hotter and hotter water until the stain is completely gone.

Of course, before you attempt this method, check what kind of fabric the garment is made of. If the stain is very large, and the product is dry-cleanable only, leave the job to professionals.

Natural fabrics are harder to clean than are man-made products. Nylon, Rayon, Dacron, Orlon, etc., need less work to clean than do cotton, linen, or wool. Pure silk should only be professionally dry-cleaned. Raw, unlined silk may be washed.

If you get a popsicle stain on a nylon windbreaker, the stain has not been absorbed into the artificial fibers, only between the spaces woven into the material. The addition of a bubbling action is helpful to work the stain out. So shaving foam works better than ordinary soap and water with a fine mesh such as nylon. Rub ordinary shaving foam—not gel—on both sides of the stain. Then rinse in lukewarm water. Repeat as often as necessary until the stain is gone.

Shaving foam is a marvelous household cleaner for cleaning your carpet, a wool overcoat, upholstery, or anywhere that the use of a lot of water is undesirable.

A listener once phoned in with a problem that only shaving foam could handle. She and her husband were on their way out the door for a fancy dinner. They were dressed to the nines. She was wearing her prized mink coat. Their darling daughter did more than wave goodbye. She gave mommy and her mink a big hug. It wasn't until they got to the party that mommy discovered, to her horror, that her beautiful mink was now wearing the dried remains of her daughter's jelly doughnut. The fur was encrusted with sugar, starch, and fruit concentrate. Fortunately, she didn't panic. She waited until the next day and phoned me on the air, asking what to do. When I told her the simple solution she was flabbergasted. But she called me back the next day to thank me for how well it worked.

Here is the procedure: Dampen a soft cloth with lukewarm water. Wring it out so it's only damp, not dripping wet. Daub the stain with the cloth, being careful not to soak the fur. As soon as the material begins to soften, take a small amount of shaving foam and apply it to the stain. Work it in carefully with your fingers. Then, with a fine-toothed comb, carefully begin to comb out the foam and residue. Work from

the back of the stain out, very gently, to avoid pulling
out the hairs. Repeat with another application of foam
if necessary, and gently wipe off excess foam with a
damp cloth. When clean, dry the fur gently with your

blow dryer set at "cool," while brushing gently with a fine bristle brush to bring out the nap of the fur.

Grass stains are some of the most stubborn of water-soluble stains, and kids love to grind grass stains into their trouser knees. You'll also find grass stains on your kitchen floor, on the carpet, and on running shoes. Here's how to give grass stains the brush off: use toothpaste.

Dampen the grass-stained fabric and use your fingers to work a dollop of toothpaste right into the stain. Work up a good lather, then rinse with cold water. Repeat the procedure several times if necessary. Bear in mind that toothpaste also contains a bleaching whitener, and it can cause colored garments to fade. Check stain section for further information.

Toothpaste is great for cleaning lots of stains. Use it with an old toothbrush for getting into those hard-to-reach places like the blades of your blender, between the grooves of your golf clubs, or removing grass stains from white leather shoes. Remove tobacco stains from ashtrays with toothpaste. It's ideal for cleaning jewelry, metal watchbands, countertops, around the bathroom sink taps, china cups and plates, even dusty figurines. The same cleaning agents and compounds that do such a good job of cleaning, whitening, and polishing your teeth have hundreds of other applications in taking the bite out of stains all around your home.

Some of the most powerful cleaning agents are acids. Don't get scared. I'm not talking about battery acid or sulfuric acid. Some of the most common household substances, such as cream of tartar and lemon juice are acidic. But my favorite cleaning acid is plain vinegar. For obvious reasons, distilled white vinegar is preferable to red wine vinegar for removing stains.

For an easily available, quick-cleaning solution, mix two parts of vinegar to one part of water. That makes a strong solution. For a milder one, use two

parts water to one part vinegar. If you mix it up in a glass jar, you can store it for use any time, for cleaning excess wax from your coffee table, for removing dirt from piano keys, and for cleaning mirrors and windows. It's also great for washing the inside and outside of your refrigerator and freezer. It's superb for cleaning the metal areas of your stove and the chrome bumpers on your car. Because vinegar is an acid, it's always a good idea to go over the area a second time with a cloth dampened in plain water, to remove the excess acid.

When cleaning the waxy buildup on a piece of furniture with the vinegar solution, don't try to do the entire large area at once. Divide the tabletop into squares or grids not much larger than eight inches square. Work on one square at a time. Apply vinegar and water with a soft, clean cloth, rubbing to remove the build-up of wax and dirt. Then dry each area with a clean, dry cloth before going on to the next square.

Keep your jar of vinegar cleaner on hand, and it will always be ready to help you out of a pickle!

So much for the good news. Water-soluble stains are easy to tackle. Now, here's the bad news. Grease and oil. Whether their source is animal, vegetable, or mineral, oil and grease stains are among the most tricky to deal with.

Suppose you drip popcorn butter onto your dress or slacks. The easiest way to remove that oily stain is to use a small can of the dry powder spray that's available at your local supermarket. But what if you don't have that product? All is not lost. The first thing to do is prevent the stain from spreading. If you are at home, apply a dry cleaner such as cornstarch, corn meal, or oatmeal (dry not cooked). This will also absorb a certain percentage of the fats and oils. Next, get a little liquid detergent or soap and rub it into the stain with your fingers. Then add a little lukewarm water, work it into the stain for a few moments, and press a blotter of folded paper towels or tissues onto the spot. This will absorb the moisture.

This procedure can be used for all minor grease and oil spots, such as gravy, margarine, and salad oil. It is an emergency-level solution. After the emergency has passed, you should drop off the garment with a professional dry cleaner.

If you want to know why your local dry cleaner is so much better equipped than you are to deal with stains, here is some behind-the-scenes information. Your dry cleaner can handle 35 and 40 pounds of material in his machine all at the same time, and the clothes don't all ball up into one mess. That is because of the dry-cleaning solvent they use. Unlike water, dry-cleaning solvent does not penetrate the fibers. This is particularly important in dealing with natural fibers such as silk, wool, and cotton. When your butter-stained garment goes into his cleaning solutions, the solvents work around and between the fibers, lifting off the grease. It's done evenly because it covers the entire area.

Here is something else you may not have known; added to that cleaning solvent is a special soap called a co-solvent, which brings the dry-cleaning solution even closer to the fibers. When the process is complete, the solutions are extracted from the clothes, which then go into a drying cycle that takes less time than your home dryer does, reducing the chances of damage and shrinkage. If you ever get your clothes back from a dry cleaner and some of them have shrunk, change to another dry cleaner. Yours is using cheap soaps.

There is another family of grease and oil stains, much more difficult than butter, cooking oil, gravy, and salad dressing stains. They are those from the vast and mysterious petrochemical industry. Automotive grease and oil stains are easy to get from fixing the lawn mower, the boat, the bicycle chain, or from oiling the sewing machine. You can even get them from the greasy water that splashes up from the road on a rainy day. And don't forget petroleum jelly and suntan lotions.

With all of these heavy greases, you may figure you'll never get them out. But they, too, will go the way of all bad stains as long as you don't panic. You must

pre-treat heavy grease stains before you wash them.

If you're outside working on a bicycle and get an oil stain on your blue jeans, here is what to do. Grab a handful of dirt or sand and pack it onto the grease spot. Then brush off the excess, once the stain has been stopped from spreading.

Don't be concerned about adding more dirt. Who cares? You're going to have to wash the jeans anyway, right?

This method works basically the same way as the cornstarch on the butter stain. Absorb excess grease and stop the stain from spreading until you're ready to clean it in your laundry.

Unless these are very expensive jeans, you probably won't be taking them to the dry cleaners. You can launder them at home. But you must be careful. Remember, the jeans are cotton denim, a natural fabric. Without pre-treating the stain, the chances of removing it from the fibers during the wash are small. Once through the washer and dryer, the heat will lock the stain right in. That is why it is very important to pre-treat those stains.

I won't name any specific brand of pre-treating products, but the shelves of your local supermarket have all kinds of them available. The majority do exactly what the manufacturer says they'll do. They're great. Some are loaded with enzymes to eat vegetable matter and grass stains. Others emulsify grease stains.

If you do not have any commercial pre-wash treating products on hand, it's simple to make one up. Here is an easy formula that will work wonders in treating heavy grease stains.

The next time you're near your local service

station, pick up a can of cleaning solvent. It's useful for lots of things, like washing off bicycle chains or cleaning your greasy tools after working on the lawn mower.

Take a tablespoonful of that cleaning solvent and three tablespoonfuls of liquid dishwashing soap, mix them together and apply them to the stain. Work them in thoroughly and put them right into the wash. Do not rinse the compound off first. You will have emulsified the grease with the combination of solvent and soap, which penetrates the fibers. When it goes into the wash, along with your favorite laundry detergent, the water, soap, and solvent all work together to float that stain right down the drain.

Homemade solutions are inexpensive and fine for stain removal on a temporary basis, or for your rugged, everyday, kick-around clothes.

But when your $600 silk dress or your fine Alfred Sung jacket are involved, for goodness' sake, avoid the heartbreak of ruining these fine and costly things. Depend on the expertise of your professional dry cleaner. As I said, they are far better equipped at dealing with these problems than you and I are. Although their services may seem expensive, consider what it would cost to replace your personal effects if you should damage them by fooling around trying to do it yourself.

At the end of this book you will find an appendix, to help in your basic laundry as well as to meet your unusual stain-removing needs. It is an alphabetical list of some common and some uncommon stains and hints on how to clean them. Interspersed are a few more general cleaning tips I have collected.

Whatever cleaning obstacle confronts you, bear in mind that you have many allies on your side. You have easy access to the world's greatest solvent, water. You have the numerous man-made contributions in the form of chemical cleaners and solvents. But the biggest help in any household emergency is what we all have but are sometimes afraid to use. That is common sense.

A Word of Warning

I do not recommend the use of such volatile liquids as white gas, kerosene, and lighter fluid. With the possible exception of rubbing alcohol, these volatile liquids are far too dangerous to store in and around the home. If you have small children who cannot read or understand safety precautions, it is a bad idea to use any of these liquids inside the home.

The hints I give you in this book depend on, with the exception of rubbing alcohol and borax, materials which are not, by themselves, dangerous, unless taken internally. There are, however, combinations of common products which can be extremely dangerous when mixed together. Some of us feel that, because one substance works well as a cleaner, why not use two substances to do an even better job? Nothing could be further from the truth when you are dealing with household bleach and ammonia. *Never combine the two.* They can produce toxic and dangerous gases which can be explosive as well as carcinogenic.

Please, before you make any decisions to clean anything at home, read the labels carefully. Unless you are an expert chemist, never improvise. Keep all chemicals, liquid or dry, in an area inaccessible to the reaching hands of curious children or grandchildren. I cannot stress this area of home safety too strongly. Our news services are filled with stories every year of the tragic loss of loved ones through sheer stupidity and carelessness in handling household chemicals.

Several times a year I get calls from listeners telling me they've heard stories that some houseplants can be dangerous. I give them a strange answer; yes and no. There are houseplants in some of our homes that, if we or our children or our pets were to chew on their leaves, could make us ill. The plants, left by

themselves, are not dangerous as long as we refrain from ingesting them. The more common variety of houseplants that can be dangerous if taken internally are dieffenbachia, philodendron, pothos, shamrock, and the sap of the poinsettia.

Out in the garden, laburnum, daphne, autumn crocus, and the leaves of the rhubarb plant can be poisonous. When preparing rhubarb stalks, always discard the leaves. They, as well as philodendron,

dieffenbachia, and shamrocks, contain oxalic acid, which, if ingested, can lead to severe kidney damage. The poinsettia has been overly maligned lately. It is actually not as dangerous as many believe. There is a sap that can be found on broken leaves and stems of poinsettias, which can cause minor skin irritation. But its effects are relatively mild. For more information on dangerous plants, contact your local poison control center. They have extensive information.

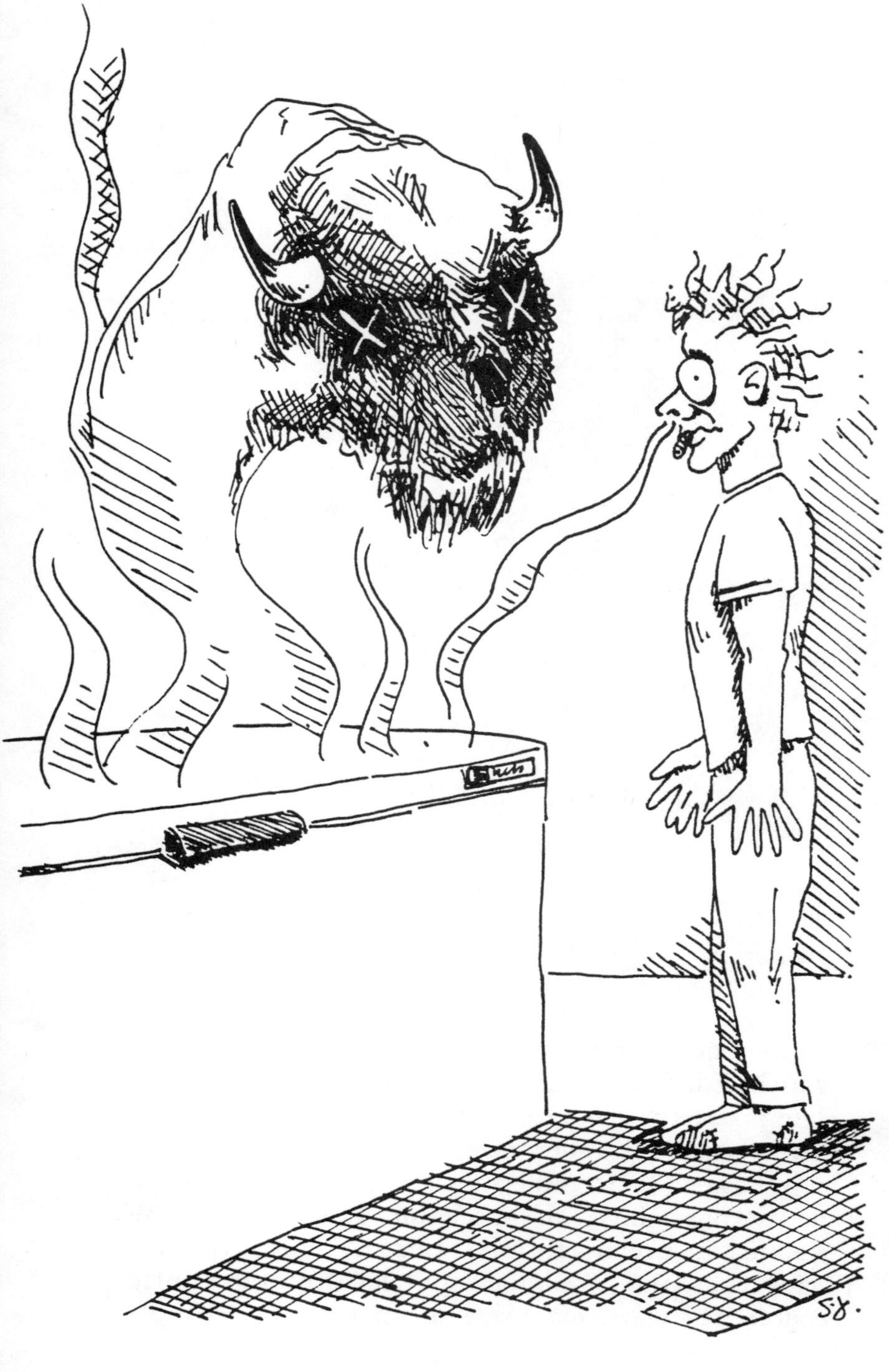

Nobody Nose My Troubles

"Go ahead line two."
"My basement smells like a dead buffalo."

I'll never forget the phone call I got on the air from a woman who had just returned home from her holidays. She said she knew something was dramatically wrong when she saw a flock of vultures circling her roof.

I said, "What died?"

She said, "My freezer."

She and her family had gone away for a three-week summer vacation. The basement freezer had somehow shut down. This poor listener had $200 worth of meat now rotting in a very expensive chest-type freezer.

The cleanup for such a problem must start as fast as possible. Put on a pair of rubber gloves and start loading the decaying meat into plastic garbage bags. It's a stinking job, literally. Once the freezer is unloaded, you can start soaking up the residual liquid.

Next, wash the inside of the freezer with a mixture made with a half gallon of water, 1/2 cup of vinegar, and 2 tablespoons of baking soda. Wash it as thoroughly as possible.

Now line the bottom of the freezer with a layer of newspapers. On the newspaper, put an unopened bag of charcoal briquets. Carefully slit open the top of the bag, opening the wrapper to expose as much of the charcoal to the air as possible without spilling charcoal dust into the freezer.

Shut the freezer lid and leave the freezer, unplugged, for 24 to 48 hours. Cross your fingers. I warn you, it's entirely possible the freezer may never recover.

The reason why success cannot be guaranteed is this. Decayed meat emits one of the most difficult of all odors to eliminate. When the freezer failed, it would have taken 24 to 36 hours for its contents to begin to thaw. Deterioration and decay would not have started for probably three days. Had the homeowner returned within that time, the freezer would probably have been OK. But after a week or ten days, the point of no return may have been passed.

If you examine your freezer you will notice that there is a lot of space between the outside and the inside walls. That thickness is filled with heavy packing insulation, which keeps the cold inside and the heat outside. But there are lots of spaces for odor to seep in with the insulation. Depending on how much odor soaked into the walls of the freezer, you may be faced with one of three alternatives.

You may have to buy a new freezer. If so, first check with your insurance agent to see if your homeowner's policy covers freezer failure. You may even be reimbursed for replacing some of the spoiled contents.

There may be a company in your area that will take your old freezer apart and replace the old insulation and packing with new, clean material. Be careful, though, because the expense of this process can be nearly as costly as buying a new freezer.

If you choose to make the best of a bad situation, be happy to learn that, once your freezer is turned back on and as time goes by, the odor will begin to diminish. You can aid the process by putting into the freezer a dish of cotton balls soaked in vanilla extract. A bowl of coffee grounds or some lemon rinds mulched up in a blender will also work to help mask the unpleasant odors.

If you are able to do so, move the freezer outside or into a garage while it is "airing out."

These procedures may also be applied when power failures affect refrigerators at home, at the cottage, or aboard boats. Use the odor treatments to freshen ice boxes and picnic coolers, too.

The spoiled-meat story points out the value of having someone check in on your home periodically while you are away for an extended time. If that is not possible, then try to use up your stored perishables before you go away. If you are able to empty your freezer first, then leave it unplugged and prop open the lid to get good circulation of air through it.

Turn down your kitchen refrigerator to its lowest setting (least amount of cooling), to maintain the flow of fluid circulating through it.

When you return from your vacation, you can re-stock with fresh meats and dairy products. I know this may be difficult, but it can save you a lot of problems in the future.

There are other problems beside freezer failure that can leave your home smelling like a dead buffalo. Old socks and running shoes; hockey equipment left zipped into an athletic bag during the off-season; baby's diapers; the drip pan under your refrigerator; the grease can below your barbecue; vegetable matter trapped in the recesses of your garbage disposal. Tobacco smoke damages more than human lungs. It invades and harms your walls, carpets, and drapes.

(How can you tell I'm a non-smoker?)

    You'd be very surprised to learn the amount of damage that tobacco smoke can do to electronic equipment. Dave Glasstetter, one of the best engineers in Canadian broadcasting, has informed me that

regular exposure of cigarette smoke to broadcasting studios can do up to $14,000 damage a year. Put that in your pipe and smoke it!

Have you got a home computer, stereo equipment, or videotape gear? If you insist on smoking

around it, at least keep it covered when you're not using it, to minimize the harmful effects of smoke and dust.

Let's talk about pet odors. What do you do if Fluffy or Fido performs a "pot au doo-doo" on your kitchen or basement floor or, heaven forbid, on the front-room carpet?

Vinegar and baking soda to the rescue once again. Remember the solution we used to clean up the freezer? This time mix a pint of water, a quarter cup of vinegar, and two tablespoons of baking soda.

First, remove any solid particles from the afflicted area. (You probably didn't need me to tell you that. Such things are as obvious as the nose on your face.)

If the accident has occurred on a non-porous

surface such as the kitchen or basement floor, first soak up the puddle with paper towels. Then wash the area down with the vinegar and baking-soda solution. If you have some, add some disinfectant such as Lysol or Dettol to the washing solution. This should more than take care of the problem.

If the accident happened on the broadloom or a rug, it is more serious. Urine on carpeting must be treated immediately. First, prepare a large blotter made from a stack of clean cloths, from two to three inches thick, large enough to cover the stained area. Pour a small amount of the vinegar and baking-soda solution onto the stain to help neutralize the acidic and ammonia effects of the urine. NEVER USE BLEACH!

Now, place the pad of clean cloths, which have first been dampened and then rung dry, onto the stain. Tamp them down with your foot. Leave it for a few minutes to soak up as much as possible. Then rinse the cloths in cold water, wring them dry, and keep re-applying the pad of cloths until you have soaked up as much as you can.

If a urine stain is allowed to stand untreated, it quickly becomes a breeding ground for bacteria. This is what causes unpleasant odor. To prevent odors, we must kill the bacteria.

Don't forget that under your wall-to-wall carpet is a spongy underlay. You must remove the urine not only from the carpeting on top, but also from the underlay below. Both need to be treated with disinfectant.

If a stain occurs close enough to a wall, you may be able to pull up the carpeting and roll it up enough to expose the stained underlay. If so, put your pad of blotting cloths between the carpet and the underlay. However, if the stain is in the center of the room, you must keep repeating the blotting process as described earlier. After four or five times, you can leave the pack of cloths on the stain for an hour at a time. You must judge how many times you need to repeat using the disinfectant, vinegar and baking-soda solution in order to neutralize the urine and bacteria. But avoid using so much liquid that you spread the stain further.

If you find your carpet is stained considerably, check out all of your carpeting. See if it isn't time for an all-over, professional cleaning job. I personally recommend that everyone's carpets should be cleaned at least once every two years. When you have laid out the kind of money it costs to install good carpeting in the first place, it only makes good common sense to keep it clean. I recommend the hot-water rinse extraction, or steam-cleaning method. When done by a professional carpet cleaner, the method is safe even for wool carpets.

After your dog or cat has had an accident, unless it is a young kitten or puppy that is not yet housetrained or accustomed to the litterbox, watch your pet very closely for the next day or two. If it appears something is the matter with your pet, consult your veterinarian. Cats, more than dogs, will have a tendency to return to the scene of the crime, and unless it is checked and stopped immediately, you could be in for long-term problems.

Unquestionably, the worst odor imaginable is the one generated by that cute little black rodent with the white stripe down its back. For some reason, dogs seem to think skunks are fun to chase. But when Flower decides to end the game by turning on Fido, it will not be long before you become painfully aware of the encounter.

To clean skunk odor off your dog, start with four or five large cans of tomato juice. Put on a pair of rubber gloves before you pick up the dog and put him into an old washtub. Pour tomato juice all over the dog, and bathe him thoroughly with it, working the juice well into the fur. The acid in the tomato juice will work as well as anything to neutralize the skunk oil.

About the only positive note I can think of is that once a dog has learned the truth about skunks, it is

most unlikely he will make the same mistake a second time. Any dog that stupid has poor survival skills and is probably not long for this world anyway.

Let's sniff out some of the day-to-day odors we come across. Every room in your home, your car, your cabin at the lake, or your boat if you are lucky enough to have one; your office, too, is filled with various odors. Some are pleasant and can bring back a lot of good memories. Who can ever forget the smell of a Sunday dinner or a special meal celebrating a family milestone or a religious event? The thrill of the scent of your first brand new car. Or what it was like the first day you walked into a new job and they showed you into a new office with a new desk and new furniture. Or the wonderful aroma of clean clothes dried the old-fashioned way, outside on a clothesline. Those are all smells that are pleasant, and I'm sure we can all identify with some of them.

But what we want to talk about in this section is the stuff we don't like. The real nose-holders!

In the kitchen, we find old grease from a dirty stove or heavy reminders of last night's fried fish. These can be dealt with quite simply and very effectively. If you do a lot of cooking, broiling, or baking, try to keep the stove as clean as you can. The appliance will operate more efficiently, and your day-to-day housekeeping chores will be easier. Once a heavy grease residue builds up in your stove, you would be surprised at how quickly that grease, when vaporized by heat into smoke, spreads odors onto your walls, curtains, and upholstery.

A really good trick in maintaining a very pleasant odor in your home is to, every once in a while, sprinkle fresh, dry coffee grounds onto a heated element of your electric stove. Or, take those cotton balls soaked in vanilla extract or a combination of fresh coffee and vanilla, and place a couple of them strategically around your kitchen, living room, or family room. These are quick and effective household deodorants.

I am sure we are all aware that there are several deodorants on the market today, be they aerosols, liquids, or solids. In some cases, the smell of some of these commercially available products can be just as offensive to some people's noses as the odors that they were trying to get rid of. In a small space, the pines can be too piny, the orchids too orkey, and the lavender can smell like a cheap back room in a Mexican cantina. Olé!

The best way to keep your kitchen garbage disposal smelling fresh is to grind up some lemon rind in it. Whenever you squeeze a lemon for its juice, don't throw away the rind. Save them in a jar or plastic bag in the freezer. You can use a twist of rind in drinks. And, once a week, grind up one in the garburator to keep it smelling nice.

You can make a mulch of lemon rinds, chopped up in your blender or food processor, as a deodorant. Orange rinds work too. Put the pieces into a pot of water left simmering on the stove. It will lend a pleasant citrus smell to the home.

During the Christmas season, try making an orange-and-clove pomander. Buy some medium-sized oranges and a bag of bulk whole cloves. Simply insert into the orange as many cloves as it will hold. Then attach a string to allow you to hang it up. Or simply place it on a shelf. As it dries, it will emit a wonderfully festive aroma. These pomanders can even make thoughtful gifts.

You can make an inexpensive but effective air freshener for your car by using a small glass jar with some holes punched through the lid. Into the jar put chopped-up lemon and orange rinds. Let the jar roll around on the back floor of the car for a day or two. Then remove it before the fruit starts to deteriorate.

The same jar with a few cotton balls soaked in vanilla extract gives you another scent of air freshener for your car or boat. One word of warning: never place any objects on the deck below a car's rear window. In a sudden stop, such objects can become deadly missiles aimed at the back of your head.

Dollars in Your Wastebasket

"Go ahead line three."

"Do you have any tips on how to save money?"

Those of us who live in North America have a reputation for creating more garbage in a lifetime than the combined gross national products of some smaller countries. Next time you're putting your garbage bags out for pickup, take a look down the alley, or into the trash bin, and see the amount of materials we throw out. Some of this can be recycled and used time and time again, right in your own home.

Glass jars, for example, in sizes varying from little jam jars to big pickle jars, are better storage containers than some of the packaging supplied by some product manufacturers. A small mustard jar is perfect for storing cloves of garlic on one of the shelves in your refrigerator door. Use a larger jar for storing whole coffee beans or ground coffee in your refrigerator.

The larger-sized jars are great for storing

leftovers. They are better than plastic because glass doesn't absorb odors.

I don't know how anyone can get by in the kitchen without the help of a couple of shaker jars. The ones I use started out holding raspberry jam and pickle relish. Now I use them for making lump-free sauces and gravies. You simply put flour or cornstarch in the jar with water or liquids, screw the lid on the jar and shake, shake, shake! Now blend it with your pan juices. I have never had a lumpy gravy nor a lumpy sauce since I started using shaker jars. Heaven forbid. And the jars didn't cost me one extra penny.

Do you need a quick salad dressing? Who needs an expensive blender or food processor? Use a shaker jar to blend vinegar, oil, and spices. I'll give you a recipe in the next chapter.

The plastic tubs that margarine comes in are also super freezer containers. If you like to prepare meals ahead, these plastic tubs make great containers for soups, stews, chilies, all kinds of leftovers, for freezing. They hold your sauces and gravies. And when berry season rolls around, they're perfect for freezer jams. You would be surprised, if you use the low-cholesterol spread as much as we do in our home, how many of these containers you collect during a few months. If you have a large family, it's a great way to get more mileage out of your shopping dollar.

Did you know there is currently a concern among health experts regarding cans? Even though our modern canning methods are dramatically different than they were during our grandparents' time, some experts feel that the exposure of our foods to metallic containers may be detrimental. I refer to foods such as canned fruits and juices which are left in tins for any length of time. In some canning processes, there may be a higher proportion of lead in the cans which, in effect, may permeate itself into the food. I am not sure at this stage how serious the problem is, but food in glass jars and other glass containers has always tasted better to me anyway.

Do you own a 35 mm camera? Don't throw away the containers your film comes in. Did you know they make fantastic carriers for your vitamins or other pills? In your car, they can carry change for parking meters. I keep one for quarters, one for dimes, and a third for nickels. They're always handy in the glove compartment.

They are super as salt-and-pepper holders and spice containers in your picnic basket, boat, or camper. They'll even hold a few Alka Seltzer tablets in your desk at work for the mornings when you bring a hangover into your office. They are excellent for holding matches dry and safe in your knapsack or galley. And they organize loose buttons, needles and pins, paper clips, tacks, and small hardware items.

You'll be amazed at how many things fit into these sturdy, moisture-proof containers. And you've already paid for them when you bought the 35 mm film. Don't throw them away.

When you go shopping today, for groceries, at the drug-store, department store, anywhere, you virtually never come back with a heavy, brown paper bag. They are things of the past. They were great for packing large lunches and even for roasting turkeys, believe it or not.

But today's modern technology has produced a whole new bag. The plastic one with handles. Some supermarkets charge a few pennies extra for them. And in the stores where you pack your own groceries, it's a good idea to bring some with you. But there are lots more uses for those plastic shopping bags after they are finished carrying their original burden.

Hung on the wall in the children's closet, they are great for collecting dirty underwear and socks. Hang them in your kitchen or laundry cupboards for keeping dust cloths and polishing rags. Hang a couple of bags up in the workshop and garage for the oily rags that were used on the lawnmower, car, or bicycle. If you happen to do a lot of sewing, knitting, or quilting, they are ideal containers for your bits and pieces of fabrics, balls of wool, and knitting needles. They are flexible, can carry a surprising weight without tearing, and can be hung up anywhere.

There is even a use for these plastic bags in your freezer. If your freezer looks disarrayed, as if an elephant herd has taken a detour through it, organize the contents with plastic shopping bags. Put all the frozen vegetables in one bag; the roasts in another; strawberries in a third, etc. Use a separate bag for fish, juices, sausages, whatever. You can tie the handles to keep the contents from spilling out, and you don't even need a twist tie!

When you barbecue, use a plastic bag hung over the handle of the barbecue as a litter bag. If you barbecue the way I do, spilling sauces and dropping and burning things, a litter bag close by is not merely handy, it's a necessity. It serves as a drop-point for failed experiments, dirty napkins, empty cans, etc.

When the weatherman warns of impending frost, use plastic shopping bags in your garden to cover small plants and bushes overnight.

Keep one in your pocket when you are going for a walk in the country. In case you find a bush of ripe berries, pick them into the bag. It's much handier than lugging around a plastic pail or bucket.

Thoughtful dog-walkers will keep a plastic bag folded in a pocket for use during outings with the pooch on public property. Put the bag over your hand like a glove. Pick up the offensive substance. Turn the bag inside out, and secure the bag tightly. Dispose of it in the nearest litter bin.

You'll find more uses for plastic shopping bags, I'm sure. So don't throw them away.

Don't throw away old socks. Wool sport socks and tube socks have a second reincarnation waiting for them as dusters and polishers. They make the greatest shoe-shining cloths in the world. Just put your hand inside and buff.

Don't throw away old towels. Besides their obvious value as cleaning and dusting rags, you can cut them into strips, if they are long enough, and tie them around your head as sweatbands when you work out.

Don't throw away your old toothbrushes. They are perfect for polishing the stainless steel on your stove. I have in my kitchen a stove that has more stainless steel per square inch than a Delorian. It is not the stove of my choice. It is just too hard to keep clean. What I really want some day is a large, commercial gas stove, because cooking is my hobby. I suppose we all dream of having a restaurant at some time in our life. But for now, I'll be content just to cook dinner for my friends.

But meanwhile, back on the range, every time I cook there is always a heavy, greasy buildup that accompanies sautéing, broiling, frying, whatever. And I cannot for the life of me get my stove clean by just using standard household cleaners and elbow grease. But I have found, and please don't laugh too hard, that the one thing that will clean my stove and almost any metal appliance beautifully is an old toothbrush, lukewarm water, and toothpaste.

Toothbrushes and toothpaste will clean your jewelry, fine filigreed silverware, grass-stains on blue jeans, the hard-to-reach corners of your shoes while you're polishing them, around the blades of your can-opener, and there's nothing better for cleaning the keys of your typewriter than an old toothbrush dipped in cleaning solvent.

It's easy for you to save lots of dollars. Hang onto some of the things you might ordinarily throw away. You'll discover numerous practical uses for lots of recyclable items. Here are two more before we shift gears: those empty pop cans and cardboard milk cartons. Next time you're going on a picnic, fill them full of water and put them in the freezer overnight. The next morning, use them instead of ice cubes to keep your cooler cold. The milk carton makes one big block of ice, and half a dozen frozen cans make a much tidier cold pack for your cooler than a bunch of jumbled up ice cubes.

By the way, did you know that one of the most effective ways to store that fish you caught over the weekend is to put it into a cardboard milk carton, fill it with water, and freeze it? The fish is locked in, frozen solid, and will not get freezer burn because it is not exposed to the air.

Kitchen Wizardry

"Go ahead line four."
"My hard-boiled eggs must be shy. They won't come out of their shells."

If I get one call like this a year, I get twenty of them. The problem of getting hard-boiled eggs out of their shells is an easy one to solve. You have to boil your eggs longer. You must create a moisture barrier between the shell and the egg itself. That way, the eggshell will peel off very easily. Let me tell you how to do it.

Add a couple of tablespoonfuls of vinegar to the water in your saucepan. Then, if the eggs crack while boiling, the whites won't extrude into the water. Put your eggs into the pan before the water comes to a boil. When the water boils, reduce the heat to medium, to avoid too much bumping around of eggs in the pan. Cook for 10 to 15 minutes at medium heat. I guarantee you that if your eggs aren't hard-boiled after this length of time, they didn't come from a chicken!

After 15 minutes, quickly remove the pan of eggs from the stove and put them in the sink under a heavy stream of cold, running water. Do not pour the hot water out first. Run the cold water on the eggs for about 5 minutes. Then allow them to sit for another 5 minutes. This whole process will take up nearly half an hour of your time, but when you are ready to peel the eggs, they'll come clean out of the shell . . . because you've created a veil of condensation between the egg white and the porous shell.

Do you know how to identify your hard-boiled eggs if you should get them mixed up with the raw ones in your refrigerator? When in doubt, give them a spin on the countertop. A raw egg will not spin, because the liquid yolk inside keeps shifting around. A simpler method to keep them straight is to mark hard-boiled eggs, preferably with a pencil. Remember, eggshells are porous. Who wants to eat a deviled egg or potato salad that tastes like ball-point or magic-marking ink?

Those of you who may be sensitive to cholesterol, or who are concerned about the fact that one egg a week can give you as much of the low-density cholesterol as some experts say your system can tolerate, may want to try using one of the egg substitutes that are now available. They are made up, primarily, of egg whites, corn oil, and other stabilizers. They are great when scrambled, or in omelets, or where eggs are called for in baking. But if you are a purist who wants the taste of that real chopped egg in a salad or sandwich, then use all the white but not all the yolk. It is largely fat, you know. Throw away all the yolk, or three-quarters, or half of it, depending on how "evil" you want to be.

By the way, do you know the difference between brown eggs and white ones? From a nutritional point of view, there is absolutely no difference. My experts tell me it actually has something to do with the breed of the chicken. (Some chickens lay blue eggs!)

You can keep fresh eggs in your refrigerator longer in a jar, or even in a pan filled with water. This way, they'll keep much better than if air were circulating around them.

Do you know why so many French recipes use so many egg yolks? It's because egg whites were used in one of the steps of the traditional French winemaking method. And chefs in frugal Chateaux kitchens needed to find uses for all the leftover yolks. You can store leftover egg yolks in a small glass jar. Add water, screw on the lid, and keep in the refrigerator for up to several days, until such time as you need them for baking custard or hardening your arteries.

Egg whites can be stored in the freezer for up to a year. Just place them in a jar or plastic container. Add to them as you collect them, or scrape out several spoonfuls as you need them. One cup equals seven egg whites. Amazingly, thawed egg whites can even be re-frozen.

Should you prefer the appearance of brown eggs to white, add onion skins to the water while you're hard boiling them. The natural pigment in the onion skins will dye the eggs brown.

Poached eggs will hold their shape better if you add a tablespoonful of vinegar to the poaching water. Crack the egg into a small cup, then slide the egg from the cup into the boiling water. When cooked, remove the poached egg with a slotted spoon.

Do you remember how elaborate and painful a process it used to be when mother or grandmother used to cook the turkey dinner? If suppertime was 6:00 P.M., the turkey went into the oven at 9:00 A.M. Mother spent all day watching the clock. She had to keep basting the bird. And there was much consternation all day about how the turkey would turn out. Luck was a necessary ingredient in the recipe, and there was a realistic fear that dinner might be tough and dry. No wonder father made such a ritual of sharpening his carving knife!

I want to share with you a fabulous way of roasting a turkey. I guarantee not only that it will give you perfect results in the form of a juicy and tender turkey, but also that it will be far easier to roast and that it will take much less time than grandmother's took. I call it Terry's Terrific Lightning Turkey. The same technique you use for turkey is also applicable for roasting chicken, duck, goose, pheasant, Cornish hen . . . any kind of poultry, except pink plastic flamingos. Your bird cooks in half the time, with practically no basting.

The method has been known for many years in fine restaurants and hotel kitchens. They simply can't afford to take as much time as grandmother did for roasting turkey. So they blanch the turkey before roasting, and then roast it at a very high temperature.

Let me give you the entire process, step by step.

First, make sure the turkey is completely thawed, if you are starting with a frozen one.

Second, prepare a large pot of boiling water. When the water is boiling, put the turkey in the kitchen sink, and pour the boiling water all over it, scalding it thoroughly, both inside the cavity and all over the skin. You will notice the skin beginning to shrink.

Next, run cold tap water all over the turkey, both inside and outside, cooling it down so you may handle it easily.

With paper towels, pat the turkey dry, inside and out.

Now you may put in the stuffing. I recommend you use a cheesecloth bag. My favorite stuffing recipe follows, on page 56. Whether or not you stuff the bird, it isn't necessary to sew the cavity together the way grandma did. Just truss the legs together. If you have stuffing left over, stuff it into the neck cavity, and secure it with a skewer.

Put the turkey on a rack in a roasting pan. The bird must be elevated, so the hot air can circulate under and around it. The best kind of wire rack is the V-shaped rack specifically designed for roasting turkey. It enables you to lift the bird from the pan easily when roasting is done.

Make sure turkey wings and thighs are not touching the roasting pan. If they are, slip small pieces of aluminum foil, oiled with cooking oil, between the turkey skin and the pan.

Next, oil the entire top surface of the bird. Corn or safflower oil have less saturated fat than peanut oil or butter. Pour several tablespoonfuls into the palm of your hand, and rub it all over the turkey.

With a large sheet of aluminum foil, make a tent that will completely seal the turkey within the roasting pan. Crimp the foil edges to the outside edges of the roasting pan, all around the entire perimeter.

Roast at 450^0. That is correct. 450^0 Fahrenheit is a very hot oven. It enables you to cut your roasting time virtually in half: instead of 30 minutes per pound, 15 to 18 minutes per pound.

One-half hour before your roasting time is over is the first time you need to baste the turkey. Remove the aluminum foil (being careful of the hot steam inside), reduce oven temperature to 325^0, and baste with a bulb baster, brush, or spoon. Baste twice more during the final half-hour.

Lightning Turkey will be juicy, tender, and perfect enough to make any professional chef proud. The same method works just as well for chicken and any other bird, as long as you first seal the skin with boiling water, oil the skin, place it on a rack in a roasting pan, cover with foil, and roast at 450^0. Chickens and smaller birds may need less than one-half hour of uncovered browning time, 15 to 18 minutes per pound holds true no matter what size your bird is.

You will save literally hours of time, and your family and guests will rave about how tasty, tender, and juicy your perfectly roasted poultry turns out, each and every time.

Public health officials have convinced me of the serious problems turkey stuffing can cause. Each holiday season, between Thanksgiving and New Year's Day, there are cases of severe illness due to food poisoning caused by improper handling of turkey stuffing. The salmonella bacteria are the culprits. They like to lurk in the middle of incompletely cooked poultry, right where you put the stuffing. So never stuff a bird the night before. Stuff it only right before you roast it. And remove all stuffing as quickly as possible after roasting. If you put the stuffing into a cheesecloth bag before you stuff it into the bird, it will be very easy to remove.

Freezing does not kill salmonella, so defrosted poultry should be treated in the same way as a fresh bird. Whenever you are working with raw poultry, remember that you may have bacteria on your hands. Once the bird is in the oven, wash your hands, utensils, and work surfaces thoroughly, in hot, soapy water. Cutting boards with porous surfaces should be scrubbed with a stiff bristle brush and disinfectant at least once a week. I recommend disinfecting with a weak bleach solution, mixed one part liquid bleach to 10 parts of water. If you have an automatic dishwasher, you may use it to clean your cutting boards, but do not let wooden boards go through the drying cycle.

I apologize if that warning sounds too heavy-handed, but I would hate to see you or anyone in your family become ill from food poisoning.

One of my most pleasant childhood memories involves Christmas dinner leftovers. I will never forget the sandwiches I feasted on, made with turkey, cranberry sauce, and my mother's wonderful sausage stuffing.

If you have tried several stuffing recipes over the years without finding the right one, let me pass along the one that has been in my family for many years. I learned it from my mother. It is practically a meal all by itself. Big and heavy, almost like a meatloaf, it is extraordinarily delicious.

Start with 3 cups of cold mashed potatoes. You don't need to add any butter, milk, or seasoning when you mash them. If you insist, use reconstituted instant potato flakes, but the real, fresh ones are better.

In a very large mixing bowl, (I use a large salad bowl) mix the potatoes with 3 pounds of raw sausage meat. Use either beef or pork sausage. But because you do not brown the sausage meat, it is important that potatoes are cool.

Mix potatoes and sausage meat with 2 medium onions, diced; ½ a loaf of day old bread, finely cubed or hand-crumbled; 1 cup of oatmeal flakes; 1 tablespoon of poultry seasoning and 2 tablespoons or more of rolled sage.

If you wish, you may also add ½ cup each of diced carrots and/or diced celery. No need to add any salt, as there is plenty of it in the sausage meat.

For the job of mixing it all together, I find that even a large, long-handled spoon is no substitute for my hands. Roll up your sleeves and dive in!

I always pack the stuffing into a bag made of cheesecloth, and put the bag into the turkey, for easy removal after roasting. You can even substitute a clean nylon stocking or piece of panty hose in place of the cheesecloth.

The stuffing recipe should be the right size to stuff a 16- to 20-pound turkey. If you have any left over, put it in a plastic bag and store it in the freezer for another day. You can stuff any poultry, pork roasts, or even a boneless leg of lamb with it. Or, try frying up stuffing patties for breakfast or brunch. You could even serve grilled stuffing-burgers!

When the turkey is all roasted golden brown, it's time to make the gravy. Removing the fat from the pan juices is much easier if you allow the fat to congeal and harden. To speed up the process, drop a few ice cubes into the pan juices. Be sure to add less liquid, then, to compensate for the melting ice.

On the Prairies in the winter, we used to put the roasting pan outside in a snowbank for half an hour, so the fat could be easily chipped off the top. You could accomplish the same thing by pouring off pan juices into a heat-resistant container, and putting it into the freezer.

For guaranteed lump-free gravy, mix water with flour or cornstarch in a jar with a tight-fitting lid, and shake it until the flour or cornstarch is completely dissolved.

Here's another shortcut roasting method, this time for meats. It is a faster way to roast beef, lamb, pork, veal, even moose or bear. Any cut of meat you would normally oven roast, uncovered at 325^0, can be roasted faster this way. It's a method that has been around for centuries. It dates back to before the invention of aluminum foil and microwave ovens. You will need a quantity of coarse salt, or Kosher salt. Not the kind of rock salt you use to melt ice on the sidewalk.

You use the salt to form a coating on the roast, similar to a clay baking pot. I promise you, the meat does not pick up an abnormal amount of saltiness.

First, brown the roast in a small amount of oil in a heated frying pan. Place the browned roast on a rack in a roasting pan and season with your favorite herbs.

Next, pour a generous amount of coarse salt in a large mixing bowl, and dampen with enough water so that it will pack together when pressed with your hands.

Pack moistened salt all over the roast and the roasting rack as well. The point is to seal the entire roast under a thick coating of salt. Be sure none of the meat is left exposed. The minimum thickness of salt should be no less than one inch, preferably 1½ to 2 inches. If the salt appears too crumbly, apply more water, patting it on with your wet hands, to make sure it will stay in place, sealing the roast.

Pre-heat your oven to 475^0 and roast the meat for 15 to 18 minutes per pound. Pork should be cooked longer. Generally speaking, the roasting time will be cut in half. Meat-thermometer temperature should register 140^0 for medium-rare beef. Roast pork must be at least 175^0.

When roasting has finished, you will find that the salt covering has baked into a hard, clay-like crust. It must be cracked open. A meat mallet, rolling pin, or any other heavy, blunt instrument will do the job.

Brush off or wipe off any excess salt crystals from the surface of the meat. You will find that when you slice the roast and serve it, with all the natural juices having been sealed in, you may even have to pass the saltshaker to some of your guests.

When cooking any meats, it is always better to hold off using any salt until cooking is completed, as presalting tends to draw the moisture out, leaving meats tough and dry.

You can speed up the roasting process for baked potatoes, by inserting a metal skewer through the length of the potato. Even a clean, large nail will work. The metal conducts heat inside the potato, so it cooks from the inside as well as from outside. Cooking time takes about 20 percent less time. (NEVER TRY THIS IN A MICROWAVE OVEN!)

One of the wildest kitchen ideas I've ever heard,

from one of my listeners, is a tip which several people
have used with great success; cooking salmon in their
automatic dishwasher. Believe it or not.

This method comes in handy when you want to
cook a fish that's too large to fit into any of your
roasting pans. You can buy large fish-poaching pans,
but they are expensive, luxury items few of us can
afford. But if you have a salmon or other large fish that
you want to poach whole, you can do it. To my eyes,
there is no more dramatic food presentation on any
dining table than a fully garnished salmon, with its
head and tail intact.

Once your fish has been thoroughly cleaned and
scaled, place it on a large sheet of heavy-duty
aluminum foil. You may wish to season the cavity with
several slices of raw onion and slices of peeled fresh
lemon. Do not use any lemon rind, for it can leave a
bitter taste.

Place a second sheet of foil on top of the salmon, leaving 3 or 4 inches of excess foil on all sides. Now seal the two pieces of foil tightly together, crimping the edges all around, making sure the seal is very tight. Now put the salmon, sealed in foil, on the top rack of your dishwasher, and set the dial to regular cycle. Leave out the detergent and the dirty dishes. The salmon rides alone, throughout the entire wash-and-dry cycle.

Before unwrapping the foil, let the salmon sit for an extra 10 to 15 minutes. This is especially important if you are going to serve it cold. The skin will peel off more easily, and the meat will slice more easily if you give it a little extra time to set.

If anyone asks how you cooked your beautifully poached salmon, tell them it was cooked by the same person who washes your dishes!

Many of the medical researchers I've spoken to recommend salmon for the health. The naturally occurring oils and fats that salmon contain are evidently helpful in reducing low-density cholesterol levels. Check with your doctor.

Here's another cooking trick from the restaurant trade, this one to save you time if you're using dried pasta. Of course, if you make your own fresh pasta, or if you can buy it fresh, there is no need to be able to cook it faster. But if you enjoy eating a lot of spaghetti, linguini, fettuccine, etc., you may be interested in knowing that you can cook it ahead of time.

Boil dried pasta until it's done to your taste. Then store it in plastic containers in your refrigerator or freezer. When the day comes that you want to serve it, just drop it into boiling water. It thaws out quickly and, in minutes, is ready for you to add your favorite sauce. This is the way many restaurants are able to prepare your pasta order so quickly.

Whether you're boiling pasta or rice, add a few teaspoonfuls of cooking oil to the boiling water. This not only prevents grains or noodles from sticking together, but it also helps to keep the pot from boiling over. The oil changes the water's surface tension, just as in the old sailor's practice of pouring oil overboard to calm turbulent waters.

You should only ever have to do this job once: season a cast-iron frying pan. Wash a new pan thoroughly, then rub the inside with a thin film of cooking oil. Put the pan into a 275^0 oven, and bake it for 15 to 20 minutes. Take it out, allow it to cool, then wipe out any excess oil with a clean cloth. Now, repeat the process. Apply another film of oil, return the pan to a 300^0 oven for 30 minutes, then remove it and let it cool. Wipe out the inside, rinse it out with lukewarm water (DO NOT USE SOAP) and dry it thoroughly. From now on, never use soap and never use hot water to clean the pan. Always cook on medium-low to medium heat and foods will not stick. If foods stick to the pan, you are using too much heat. Clean stubborn stains with lukewarm water, elbow grease, and a webbed, plastic scrubber. Never use steel wool or abrasive scouring materials. And don't spray a cast iron pan with nonstick coatings. They'll ruin the surface.

Nonstick coatings are very useful on stainless steel and other washable pans. They are especially helpful for people who are trying to cut down on calories. But be careful to keep nonstick sprays out of the reach of children. Inhaling the oily spray can seriously damage lungs.

If you are fortunate enough to have a microwave oven, remember that regular cleaning is most important for efficient operation. Tiny bits and pieces of sizzling meats and spattering vegetables stick to the oven interior every time you use it. These particles can cause uneven heating, and can even lead to damage. Use a damp, clean cloth and nothing else but elbow grease to clean inside your microwave oven—at least twice a week. Even if it looks clean, give it a good wipe. You can scrape off stubborn spots with a rubber or plastic spatula. Never risk scratching by using anything metallic.

Do you have a bag of brown sugar in your cupboard which has turned into a rock-solid lump? Tuck a single slice of fresh bread into the bag of sugar and re-seal it. The moisture from the bread will soften the sugar again.

When adding salt or spices to steaming pots or pans, never shake the container of seasoning directly into the pot. The rising steam will get into the shaker and cause it to clog up; and moisture in your dried spices will deteriorate them very quickly. The reason they were dried is to make them keep longer. Shake them over a steaming saucepan and they could do more than lose their flavor. They could go moldy.

If you have any spice bottles with shaker lids under the screw tops, throw the shaker lids away. Then use a measuring spoon or shake the spices into the palm of your hand before adding them to the recipe. Not only will the spices last much longer, but you will be much less likely to accidentally dump in too much.

If you do make a mistake and put too much salt into a recipe, try counteracting the salt by adding a few drops of vinegar. Too much salt in soups or stews can be repaired by putting in a raw potato. It will absorb the extra saltiness as it cooks.

Salt can be helpful in cutting down the smoke and grease in your broiler pan. When you are broiling steaks or burgers and aren't planning to make gravy with the pan juices, pour ½ cup of salt over the bottom of the broiler pan. It will absorb the dripping grease and fat. When you are finished broiling, simply brush the salt into the garbage. Your pan will be easier to clean, and you will have reduced spattering and smoke.

Would you like to know a secret that will help you make dozens of recipes, from sauces to desserts, quickly and easily? I'll tell you the secret in one word: cornstarch.

For simple chocolate pudding without using a

packaged mix, for low-calorie sauces or rich gravies, for glazes and custards, cornstarch makes them all possible.

Here is a recipe for a quick and delicious chocolate pudding you can make from scratch. It contains no eggs, and is very low in calories and cholesterol.

  3 cups skim milk
  2 tablespoons cocoa powder (not instant drink mix)
  1/4 cup corn syrup or honey
  3 tablespoons cornstarch
  water

In a shaker jar, mix the cornstarch with ¼ cup of water and shake thoroughly until all lumps are gone. Set aside.

In another shaker jar, mix the cocoa powder with ½ cup of water until all lumps are gone. Pour into a medium saucepan and bring to a low boil, stirring occasionally, until cocoa powder is dissolved and mixture becomes less cloudy.

Add milk and corn syrup or honey. (If you use granulated sugar, stir it in until dissolved before adding milk.) Cook over medium heat, stirring constantly until you see steam rising from the mixture.

Give your shaker jar of cornstarch and water a few more shakes, then pour a small amount into the saucepan. Cook, stirring until mixture thickens. Depending on how thick or thin you want it to be, add more or less of the cornstarch and water mixture. A thin chocolate sauce to pour over pound cake or trifle will use only about one-third of the cornstarch. If you want it to set like a pudding so you can serve it in a bowl, use the full amount.

By changing the sweeteners and flavorings, this basic recipe serves as the basis for all kinds of quick sauces and puddings. Delete the cocoa and add 1/2 teaspoonful vanilla or lemon extract. Or add no flavorings and you have a white sauce to dress up fish and vegetables.

To make a lemon sauce for fish, leave out the sweetener and add some grated lemon rind and 1/2 teaspoon of salt.

Omit the milk and use vinegar and brown sugar to make a classic sweet-and-sour sauce.

Make orange sauce for roast duckling by flavoring the sauce with orange juice. The variations are endless. The bottom line is 3 cups of milk or liquid to 3 tablespoons of cornstarch for maximum thickness; 1 to 1½ tablespoons of cornstarch for minimum thickness. Just make sure you cook until the mixture turns clear. Otherwise, it will taste starchy because it won't be fully cooked.

What do you do when you discover, at the last minute, that your trusty box of cornstarch or bag of flour is empty? You can still thicken a gravy or sauce without flour or cornstarch. Simply substitute fine, dry breadcrumbs, or even finely scrunched-up pieces of fresh bread.

You can make a sweet and tangy sauce for Oriental foods or German sauerbraten by using finely crumbled gingersnap cookies as the thickening agent.

And speaking of ginger, here's a recipe for a baked-ham baste that's ready in a snap. Just open up a bottle of ginger ale. It gives a wonderful spicy flavor.

If you want to go to a little extra effort, score the top of the ham into a hatched diamond pattern, and insert whole cloves into the intersections. Mix a tablespoonful of prepared mustard and two tablespoonfuls of corn syrup with one cup of ginger ale. Spread it over the top of the ham and, while it bakes, baste the ham with the remains of the bottle of ginger ale.

Want to go whole hog? After the ham is baked, pour off the liquid from the roasting pan into a saucepan, and add: the juices of one fresh orange and one fresh lemon; up to one cup of ginger ale, if any is left; one-quarter cup of raisins; one-half of an orange rind, chopped; one-quarter of a lemon rind, chopped. You should have about three cups of liquid in the pan. If the combination of ham juices and ginger ale was not sufficient, then add orange juice to bring the liquid up to 3 cups.

Heat the mixture to boiling, then reduce heat and simmer, uncovered, 20 to 25 minutes. Finally, thicken it with that good old blend of cornstarch and water from your trusty shaker jar. You will have a delicious, tangy citrus-and-raisin relish to serve with your baked ham.

Everybody knows there's no such thing as a free lunch, but here's a recipe that comes pretty close. It's not totally fat-free and cholesterol-free, but I would not hesitate to recommend it for anyone who is trying to cut down on fats. On the other hand, if you want to throw caution to the winds, then use whole fresh eggs and whole milk instead of the egg substitutes and skim milk in the recipe. It's a quick recipe for eggplant parmesan.

Slice an eggplant into rounds about half an inch thick. Sprinkle them lightly with salt on both sides, then put them onto paper toweling for an hour to absorb the liquid. Meanwhile, prepare a dip of egg substitutes, equivalent to two eggs, one-half cup skim milk, and one-half teaspoon of celery salt. Beat the mixture to blend well. Rinse salt off eggplant rounds with cold water. Dip rounds in milk mixture, then coat both sides liberally with fine, dry bread crumbs. Add a quarter cup of olive or any cooking oil to a heated frying pan and quickly sauté eggplant slices until brown on both sides. Place eggplant in a baking dish and pour over them a 14-oz. can of Italian-style tomato sauce or meatless spaghetti sauce.

Bake in a 350⁰ oven for 30 minutes. Then remove from oven, top slices with 2 cups of shredded mozzarella cheese and ½ cup grated Parmesan cheese. Return to oven for 15 more minutes. "That's-a-Nice-a."

Finally, I hope you have saved up your empty

glass jars, because I haven't forgotten to give you a couple of recipes for homemade shaker-jar salad dressings. To my taste buds, these salad dressings are more flavorful than most commercially available bottled dressings. And the added advantages are that they are less expensive, and very quick to prepare.

For Tarragon/Mustard dressing, add the following to a shaker jar: 1 teaspoon dried tarragon leaves, 1 tablespoon Dijon mustard, 6 tablespoons salad oil, 2 tablespoons lemon juice, ½ cup water, and 1 teaspoon liquid corn syrup or honey, or 1 teaspoon sugar. Shake well. For a milder-strength dressing, add more water and oil.

Dill/Curry dressing uses 1 cup water, 1 teaspoon dried dill weed, 1 tablespoon honey or sugar, 6 tablespoons salad oil, ½ teaspoon black pepper, ½ teaspoon salt, ¼ teaspoon curry powder, and either the juice of 1 lemon or 2 tablespoons of vinegar. For a creamier version, add 1 egg white. Shake it all up in your shaker jar.

Peanut Butter On Your Head

"Go ahead line five."
"Help me, please. My daughter has a great wad of
bubble gum stuck in her hair."
"Have you tried peanut butter?" I asked.

There was silence at the end of the line. I could
imagine her silently mouthing the words, "He's nuts."
That may well be true, but I'm not crazy when I tell you
that peanut butter works like magic for removing gum
from children's hair. As a matter of fact, peanut butter
will work for removing the sticky residue left by
masking tape or cellophane tape, in addition to
cleaning out bubble gum and chewing gum from
children's hair and pets' fur.

The biggest drawback with peanut butter is that it
can get a little messy. There are a lot of solids in the
peanut butter that do you no good. It is the oil in the
peanut butter that actually lets you dissolve the gum.
And you could get the same results with less fuss by
using straight cooking oil, whether it be corn,

safflower, olive, palm, or peanut oil. Even mineral oil will give you the same result. But if all you have handy is peanut butter, and if Johnny or Sally has a big glob of gum stuck in his or her hair, merely rub the afflicted area with a generous dollop of peanut butter. Crunchy or smooth makes no difference.

Work the peanut butter into the gum with your fingers until you feel the gum beginning to ball or pill. When it starts to feel that the gum is loosening its grip from the hair, use an old comb to pull the gum away from the hair.

Finally, shampoo to remove the excess oil-and-peanut residue from the hair.

Should you find a leftover wad of gum parked underneath a table, or stuck to your carpeting (as long as it hasn't been ground in), place a couple of ice cubes in a small plastic bag and apply the ice pack to the gum. Give it a few minutes to harden, and you should then be able to lift it away easily.

The technique is useful for cleaning candlewax from your table, tablecloth, clothing, or carpet.

If you want to prevent candles from being too drippy, put them into the freezer for two hours before lighting them. They will burn more efficiently and will tend not to drip as much.

Before we get too far away from peanut butter, though, I want to throw a quick peanut butter recipe at you. It is for a simple but delicious peanut butter sauce to serve with lamb, chicken, or pork, either roast or grilled kabobs. Many people think these exotic sauces are expensive and difficult to make, but nothing could be further from the truth. You probably have all the necessary ingredients in your kitchen cupboards right now.

1/2 cup peanut butter (smooth or crunchy)
1 1/2 tablespoons prepared mustard (ordinary or fancy)
1 clove of garlic, minced or pressed
3 tablespoons soy sauce
1/2 teaspoon black pepper

Mix all the ingredients thoroughly and store in a tightly sealed glass jar. This recipe makes a large quantity, but it will keep in your refrigerator for quite a while. This simple-to-prepare but exotic-tasting peanut sauce is an Indonesian recipe, ideal for lamb, chicken, and pork.

Peanut butter is not the only food product which can double as a cleaning tool. That same mayonnaise that gives a lift to your sandwiches, burgers, and salads can also be used to remove those sticky labels and price tags from glassware, mirrors, and new plate-glass windows.

I first learned about mayonnaise as a cleaner when a listener called in for help cleaning her bathtub. She had rented an apartment where the previous tenant had stuck those ghastly rubberized, non-skid, flower-shaped decals all over the inside of the bathtub. My caller could not figure how to remove the decals without scratching the tub.

It wasn't long before another listener offered this unconventional but effective solution: mayonnaise. Smear it thoroughly over the decal, and cover it with a sheet of clear, plastic wrap to seal in the moisture. Let it sit for an hour or two. After that time, you can use a plastic ice scraper or a wooden spatula to scrape the softened glue and plastic away, without scratching the porcelain surface of the tub.

I agree 100 percent with my listener. There is no way I would have those stickers on my bathtub. They collect dirt and soap scum after a very short time and start looking grungy. They are more trouble than they are worth. If you really want something for the bottom of your bathtub, invest in a good-quality rubber mat. You might even check into the possibility of having the bottom of your bathtub treated with a nonskid process. Your local plumber will be able to give you more information.

Have you ever stuck a political candidate's sticker on your car's chrome bumper and then, after the election, been embarrassed that you couldn't peel it off? Try using mayonnaise again.

Removing paint and ink from your skin can be especially difficult if you have skin that is sensitive to harsh chemical solvents. This tip doesn't work as well for latex paint as it does for oil-based paints, ballpoint-pen ink, tar, and the like. Try removing these substances from your face and skin by rubbing cooking oil into them.

If the stain still won't come off, then mix a solvent such as paint thinner or turpentine two-to-one with cooking oil. Once the stain is gone, wash your skin thoroughly. If you have highly sensitive skin, apply a medicated cream to counteract the harshness of the chemical solvent.

Misty bathroom mirrors and foggy glasses are nothing to get steamed up about. The problem of condensation obscuring windows is a common one to people who live in the colder parts of North America; the Canadian prairies, the U.S. midwest, wherever winter brings ice and snow.

Even in the more temperate coastal climates, winter rains can leave our windows fogged in.

You have probably seen people selling products to prevent glass from misting over. They are common sights at local exhibitions, state and county fairs. I am sure you remember seeing a pitchman hawking a product called something like "Fog Proofer." He guaranteed it would eliminate condensation on the windows of your car or boat, your glasses, bathroom mirrors, and any glassy surface prone to fogging up. And he was entirely correct.

The only problem is, if you bought that "Fog Proofer," you paid a small fortune for something you already had in your home. You bought a bar of soap, with a bit of dye to color it. That's the bad news. The good news is that if your "Fog Proofer" has been used up, or if you refrained from buying it in the first place, any bar of soap you have at home will work just the same way.

There are several anti-foggers on the market, in

spray and liquid form as well as solids. But none is any more effective at combatting condensation than a cheap bar of simple soap.

How to use it may bring back some childhood memories. Remember soaping your neighbor's windows on Halloween night? You didn't? Neither did I. But I read somewhere how to do it. Take a bar of soap and draw a bunch of squiggly lines with it on the surface you want to treat. Then, with a soft, dry cloth, polish it into the glass in a circular motion until no traces of the soap are visible. That's it. The treatment will last for several weeks. Use it to keep your bathroom mirror or the inside of your ski goggles or scuba mask from steaming up. Anyone who drives a Volkswagen Beetle will find this tip a true blessing, because you will never again have to drive with one hand while mopping off the inside of the windshield with your other hand.

The next time you go to the fair and see a salesman offering a little chunk of colored soap for three or four dollars, you can feel really good that you bought this book.

Soap—liquid detergent, actually—is the best lubricant to use in removing a ring from a swollen finger. Use cold water to reduce the swelling, and liquid soap to slide the ring off.

I am forever getting my glass measuring cups stuck together. Applying a little liquid soap lets them slip apart without breaking. The same holds true for glass tumblers or china cups you have nestled together, which then become difficult to separate.

Bar soap is a good lubricant to help you make screws go into wood more easily. It also is great on smoothing out sticky drawer tracks. And use soap to make the zippers on your wetsuit slide more easily, if you are a windsurfer or scuba diver.

In some books of household hints, you will see suggestions for using hairspray to remove various stains such as ballpoint pen and marker ink. Hairspray can be useful if you do not have the one simple ingredient within the hairspray which actually does the work of removing the stain. It, alone, is a lot cheaper, too. It's alcohol. Keep a bottle of ordinary rubbing alcohol handy in your bag of household cleaning tricks. It's a great solvent for removing shoepolish, both liquid and paste kinds; ink, crayon marks from walls, and lipstick marks on both hard surfaces and fabrics.

You can make a very good furniture cleaner by mixing 2 parts cooking oil, 2 parts turpentine, 1 part vinegar, and ½ part rubbing alcohol. Use it sparingly on sticky or dirty marks on your furniture. It works on varnished, shellacked, or oiled wooden surfaces. (See *Furniture* in Appendix.)

For example, if the company you had for dinner

last night spilled gravy or rum sauce onto your dining table, or if someone's liqueur left a sticky residue on the coffee table, use this cleaner. Apply a small amount of it with a soft cloth. Work on only a small area at one time, and wipe it off immediately, to avoid leaving any white marks behind on the wooden surface.

Pity our poor bathrooms. Over the past several years, bathrooms have been the worst-designed rooms in our homes and apartments. They suffer from inadequate ventilation and poor air circulation. As a result, we have to put up with mold and mildew.

Fortunately, times seem to be changing as some builders and designers realize that attention must be paid to practicality as well as to aesthetics, and that the rooms we visit four times every day require air and sunlight. Without them, our bathrooms are breeding grounds for a major household cleaning problem, mildew.

Mildew is a living organism, a fungus-like growth that occurs on shower curtains, in the grout between tiles and around the tub, even on walls and ceilings. It is not only unsightly, it is unhealthy. These moldy cells grow very rapidly, especially where the air is humid and stale, and where sunlight seldom penetrates.

If you are lucky enough to have a bathroom with a skylight and windows that open to the outside, you are unlikely ever to have a mildew problem. But if your bathroom, like mine, is super-enclosed, there are several things you must do to combat mildew.

Keep your overhead fan on as much as possible, up to two hours after you have taken a shower. Keep the door open as well. A small fan, such as the tiny ones that fit on car dashboards, can be tucked away on the corner of the vanity to help keep air circulating.

What if these precautions are insufficient to keep that ugly mildew growth away? Today's modern spray cleaning foams work quite well to remove surface mildew and soap films. But in a small, enclosed area, where there is a nearly constant combination of soap scums, body oil, high temperatures, and lots of humidity, do not be surprised if foam cleaners do not kill off all the mildew spores. Any few remaining spores will quickly begin to multiply again. This is a job for some killer liquids. Common household bleach works well, when applied with a good bristle brush, accompanied by some elbow grease. Wear rubber gloves and don't scrub so hard you scratch the surfaces. Sudsy ammonia does a good job, too. I don't recommend using straight household ammonia, because the fumes can become overpowering in a poorly ventilated area. Household disinfectants, such as Lysol and Dettol, and some of the stronger commercially available cleaners, also help kill mildew. A once-a-week cleaning is my personal recommendation to stop mildew problems in a poorly ventilated bathroom.

If your plastic shower curtain becomes mildewed, you can wash it in your washing machine. In addition to your favorite detergent, put several large towels into the machine with the plastic shower curtain. During the wash cycle, the towels will work like scrubbers to help it get clean. You can even put the plastic shower curtain into your automatic dryer. Make sure the temperature is set on "air" only. Use no heat, and throw a couple more towels in with the curtain. Use only clean, dry towels this time. Let them spin for 10 to 15 minutes before you take the curtain out and hang it back up. A word of caution: do not use bleach or strong chemicals when you wash a plastic shower curtain. It will deteriorate. Similarly, keep bleach away from your rubber bathmats and rubber-backed bathroom rugs.

Some designer bathrooms have fabric shower curtains that hang in front of clear plastic liners. How dare any mildew have the audacity to attack anything so fancy? If the unthinkable does happen, pre-treat the mildew spots on a fabric shower curtain with a commercial pre-wash solution that contains enzymes.

Plus, add ½ cup of household disinfectant (but not bleach) along with the detergent for the wash cycle.

On white fabrics, you may use a small amount of household chlorine bleach in the wash, too. I have found, however, that borax is a very good bleach. Remember the old TV show, "Death Valley Days," starring Ronald Reagan? The same borax which took twenty mules to haul it out of the desert will work today to haul the stains out of fabrics. And borax is much safer on a wider variety of fabrics and colors than chlorine bleach is. Not that chlorine bleach won't whiten whites, but it is no laundry-room cure-all.

Just when you thought it was safe to come out of the bathroom, we find more mildew lurking in other musty corners. The basement, the boat, storage trunks, even in the trunk of the car. Mildew can occur in just about any dark, damp place with poor air circulation.

Picture in your mind a sports bag. After the last day of the season, your pro-ball prospect stuffed his sweaty shirt, shorts, socks, and assorted gear into the zipper bag, and promptly forgot about it for the next three or four months. I guarantee, the mold and mildew growth on those towels, running shoes, etc., will be bigger, tougher, and stronger than any first-round draft choice to be signed by any professional league.

You can avoid mildew by never putting anything away damp. Make sure storage areas are dry, with room for air to circulate. Instead of piling up cardboard cartons on the floor of the garage or against the basement wall, lay two-by-fours on the floor first, so air may circulate underneath. And leave a gap of at least a few inches between the boxes and the wall.

If there is an electrical outlet accessible, invest in a small heater-fan to keep garages or basements from becoming spawning grounds for mildew. You can keep boats, campers, and recreational vehicles free of mildew by hooking up a heating-lamp bulb to a timer switch. This can be especially helpful during those long, cold, damp, dark winter evenings when they are sitting unused.

A comparatively new product is now available which may be obtained from some marine-supply companies and recreational-vehicle dealers. It is a moisture absorber, a clever little contraption that looks like a small plastic lantern. There is an area for holding chemical pellets, which look like little white beads. And there is a catchbowl for the moisture. These relatively inexpensive gadgets are designed to hang in confined areas where you want to reduce the humidity. They could save you a lot of money in the long run.

In the event you do find mildew inside your boat or other vehicle, follow the same procedure as outlined for cleaning bathroom walls.

Some people find they are unusually sensitive to mold and mildew. If you feel that such fungus growths cause unusual sneezing, sinus truouble, or even lung discomfort, check with your doctor or an allergy specialist. You can't be a fun guy if you're bothered by fungi.

What's Bugging You?

"Go ahead line six."
"There are some flying insects going in and out from under my garage roof. Are they dangerous?"
"Are they bigger than bees? Shiny black or dark brown? With fairly large wings and very slender waists?"
"Yes. What should I do?"
"Stay inside, close all doors and windows, and phone an exterminator."

My advice may not have been what he wanted to hear. But wasps and hornets are very dangerous insects. And they are also very ingenious. If you see them flying under your roof, siding, eaves, garage, or anywhere, do yourself a big favor. Call in the services of a professional exterminator. All too often I hear or see news reports on the radio, television, or newspapers about people who have been fatally stung while trying to remove a nest from their house.

Some individuals cannot tolerate even one sting. And the expression "mad as a hornet" is indeed a valid one. When these dive-bombers zero in on you, if they perceive you as a threat to their nest, they can be relentless.

If you should be living in a remote area where no expert pest-control professionals are available, I will tell you a method which may be tried as a last resort.

If the nest is under construction, wait until it has been completed. Wasps and hornets seldom fly at night, so delay your attack until at least an hour after sunset. Arm yourself with a strong flashlight, an aerosol can of flying-insect spray, and a large, green plastic garbage bag. Wear gloves and long-sleeved clothing that leaves the minimal amount of skin exposed as a target.

Build a small fire, preferably in a metal container such as an old garbage can or wash tub. Or dig a hole in the ground away from overhanging branches and build the fire in that. Make it sufficiently large and hot that there will be a good flame.

Now, cover the nest with the garbage bag and quickly cut it loose from its anchor, using a large knife or some other sharp metal object. Immediately seal the bag with a twist tie and throw it into the fire. Fire your aerosol spray at any insects that escape.

If the nest is located inside the walls of your house or garage, try to watch where the pests enter and exit. People have tried to spray insecticides into these holes and then seal them with grease or wax, but it is probable the intruders have several "doors." And it is unlikely the insecticide spray will reach into all the chambers of the nest. You will need good luck. In the meantime, keep children and pets away from the area.

Wasps and hornets have a highly developed sense of smell. Perfumes, aftershave lotions, and colognes attract them. So do cooking odors, and you will often see them around your platter of chicken or burgers by the barbecue. Even some unpleasant scents seem to draw them in. And the best way to free yourself from an invasion of these flying hazards is to call an exterminator. He won't sting you nearly as badly as they can.

There are other little creatures which will bug you, but are not nearly as dangerous to your life, although they can be very destructive. Ants, as a matter of fact, can eat you literally out of house and home. On the West Coast, large carpenter ants have been known to cause seemingly perfectly good houses to be condemned by eating the wooden support beams and rafters to the point where they were ready to collapse.

Once carpenter ants have a foothold, they can be very difficult tenants to evict. You can spray, put out bait until you are blue in the face, but those measures will not adequately deal with an active nest of carpenter ants. You need a professional exterminator to fumigate your house.

In the east, where brick and cement are more common house-building materials than wood, carpenter ants are far less of a problem. But termites do pose a major threat to those homes which do use wood, especially in the south.

Should you be unable to get the help of a professional pest-control expert to help rid you of termites or carpenter ants, I will give you some tips that have been known to work on both small red ants and the larger, more destructive varieties. Keep in mind that they don't devour wooden homes looking for food. Just like the Boll Weavil in the old song, they are "just a-lookin' for a home." They bore tunnels in wood as places to build nests. They like to eat tastier morsels than rafters and beams. Lucky for you, because you can put out honey or corn syrup as bait...bait which you can mix with poison.

Get some boric acid from your drugstore. (In some areas it is known as borasic acid.) Mix it, in a bowl, with enough honey or corn syrup to make a pliable dough. Locate the paths on which the ants travel to and fro, and near them strategically place chunks of the poisoned bait. They will take it back to their nests. Over time, their population will diminish.

Similar ant traps and poisons are available at hardware and drugstores. These materials work much better than the insecticide sprays, which kill only the ants on the surface, not those in their nests.

Meanwhile, back in the kitchen, you open the cupboard door, peek into a bag of flour or a box of cornstarch, and—what are those tiny little brown things crawling around? Or flying around? Welcome to the wonderful world of grain beetles. Ya! Ya! Ya!

Over one hundred years ago, the theory of spontaneous generation was used to explain how grain beetles were capable of suddenly appearing inside tightly sealed containers of flour and various grains. Today we know that microscopically small eggs can be present in the cereal products we buy.

Fortunately, grain beetles won't do you any serious harm. They may, for all I know, be a good source of protein. But I do not question that, for squeamish people especially, they can be very unpleasant.

If you find grain beetles anywhere in your kitchen, you can safely bet that they have invaded almost everywhere. The most effective way to get rid of them is to throw away every single open box or bag of cereal, flour, rice, granola, cookies, crackers, dried vegetables, peas, lentils, and anything else that may be a possible food for these pernicious pests.

Throw the food away into a heavy-duty garbage bag and, before you seal it tightly, spray inside it with a good dose of insecticide.

Next, thoroughly wash your drawers and cupboards, inside and out, with a mixture of sudsy ammonia, water, and boric acid. Try to work the solution well into all the tiny crevices and cracks around the back and side edges of cupboard shelves. Remember, you are dealing with a foe whose eggs are too small for the naked eye to see.

Spraying with an aerosol insecticide would probably be the most effective cure. Spray, then shut

the cupboards for a few hours. Then carefully wash off any residual insecticide before you re-stock shelves with food.

Grains and cereal products tightly stored in glass or plastic containers will be less likely to attract grain beetles than food in paper bags or cardboard cartons. Throw away the original wrappings. And be sure to wipe up any spills of flour or crumbs whenever they occur, rather than letting them accumulate and attract unwanted houseguests.

If your infestation of grain beetles appears to be just starting, and you are reluctant to chuck out your entire pantry, you can try this simple trick before taking drastic measures: sprinkle cayenne pepper around the inside of the cupboard where you first discover any grain beetles. And, of course, destroy the package of food product in which you find them. I know how powerful cayenne pepper can feel on my tongue, and I can imagine how powerful it may feel on theirs. If these insects haven't yet got all six of their feet in your door, it just might do the trick.

Several years ago, I lived in a beautiful area in West Vancouver. The house was within a short walk of the beach, and very much in tune with nature. We were very fond of the wildlife nearby, from the menagerie of local cats and dogs, to the songbirds in the trees and the majestic eagles we occasionally would see soaring high overhead. And once in a while we would get a visit from that charming and handsome-looking creature with the ringed tail and the black mask. I confess that I actually enjoyed these nocturnal prowlers for a while.

Then came the time when I wanted to redo the landscaping. My lawn was looking awfully shabby. It looked green from across the road, but closer inspection revealed far more green moss and weeds and clover than grass. So I decided the simplest solution was to replace it all with fresh new sod.

Although the house was not all that big, I was amazed at how much larger my lot suddenly became. And the more old lawn I dug up, the larger it seemed to grow. So I hired some people to help me complete the job. There were yards and yards of gravel, sand, and earth to haul, shovel, spread, and roll smooth. There were yards and yards of sod to lay and roll and water. It took us several days of strenuous work. But the new lawn looked spectacular!

On the morning of the second day after the

landscaping, I looked out at my new lawn with horror. It was a mess. The new sod had been ripped up, overturned, and scattered all over the yard. I am sure you have guessed who the vandals were. Rocky Raccoon and his friends. After getting it all put back into place, tamped and rolled down again, I began my transformation into a great white hunter. It was quiet. Too quiet. I knew the raccoons were up to something. But I didn't know what. I waited to ambush them, but they wouldn't return until I got tired and went to bed.

Whenever I relaxed my surveillance, they would return, to hunt for the worms and grubs that were easy pickings under the fresh, damp sod.

I hired professional exterminators. I bought traps to catch them (alive). I transported 15 of them up into the mountains where I released them far away from newly sodded lawns. My neighbors accused me of being an animal hater. For weeks on end the battle raged. By night I trapped raccoons, and reinforcement raccoons came into my yard to rip up the sod. By day I replaced the sod and carried trapped raccoons up the the mountains. Finally, the raccoons won. My patience ran out. I sold the house.

I now live in an apartment. I no longer have to take care of the lawn. I no longer have to fight with raccoons.

Recently, one of my former neighbors phoned to tell me that raccoons have targeted his house now. This used to be one of the neighbors who laughed at my plight, and who said I should leave those cute little creatures alone. Now, those cute little creatures have torn holes in his roof, and are building nests in his attic. I suspect he may be considering moving into my apartment.

I tell you these stories for the purpose of informing you of the raccoon problem that has developed in many major urban areas in North America. Raccoons may look cute, but they are wild animals. They hang around areas where humans interfere with the balance of nature by feeding them, sometimes deliberately, but more often accidentally. We leave out dishes of pet food overnight. Or we leave garbage containers poorly secured. Raccoons can be highly aggressive and dangerous to pets, to children, and even to you and me. They are not only big and strong, but they are also remarkably intelligent. Stay away from them. Come to think of it, as strong and as smart as raccoons are, I probably should simply have hired them to redo my lawn.

Thyme Saving Tips and Sage Advice

"Go ahead line seven."

"My spices don't smell right, and they're not that old."

"Don't tell me. Let me guess. Is your spice rack up over your oven?"

"Can you see me through the radio? How did you know?"

Nine times out of ten, when I get complaints from listeners concerning the quality of a product they have just bought, the fault does not lie with the product; it lies with the consumer, who used it incorrectly or, in the case of the rancid spices, failed to store them correctly.

Dried herbs are one of Nature's first convenience foods. You can simply pick them from your garden when the leaves are mature, hang them carefully to dry, and cook with the dried herbs all winter, until the fresh ones return in the spring.

More commonly, you buy a bottle or jar of dried thyme or tarragon from the supermarket, but the

principle is the same. Because the herbs are dried, they retain their flavors and aromas. Dried oregano leaves, stored in a sealed container at room temperature, will last about four months. But store the same container in the heat that builds up near your oven, and the shelf-life goes down drastically. Moisture, in the form of steam from boiling pots on the range top, kills dried herbs even faster than heat.

For maximum shelf-life, I recommend you store dried herbs and ground spices in the freezer. As long as they stay dry, your sage, cinnamon, and other seasonings will keep for a year in the freezer. Granted, a spice shelf on the kitchen wall is handier, but how often during the day do you need a tablespoonful of basil, anyway?

You can save a lot of money buying herbs and spices if you have access to a market that sells them in bulk. There is no point in buying a one-ounce bottle of dried sage leaves or a two-ounce jar of ground cumin seed unless you do an enormous volume of exotic cooking. Never buy more than you will use in three months. For most home cooks, this is about one-quarter the quantity found in the average little herb or spice bottle. That is why bulk spices can be such a big money-saver. But you must resist the temptation to scoop up more than you can use before the herbs go stale. Ignore the large scoops and enormous bags some bulk-spice markets provide you. In most cases, one-half an ounce is plenty.

I have found, in comparing costs, that the cost per ounce of bulk spices can be less than half the cost of buying them already put up in jars. If your bulk-spice store has a high turnover of its stock, chances are good their products are fresher than the ones in the jars. And as long as you buy only as much as you actually will use, buying bulk herbs and spices will save you a healthy pocketful of money.

When you get home from the bulk store, transfer your half-ounce of thyme into that old mustard jar you've previously washed and dried thoroughly. Store it in your freezer. Then, in six or eight months when you use the last quarter teaspoonful of it in your stuffed butterfly porkchops, it will have lost very little of its flavor and aroma.

Bulk buying is not the only way to save money at the grocery store. If you don't have any bulk stores in your area, you can save a significant percentage of your shopping bill by avoiding impulse purchases. Plan your shopping first. Take a few minutes to look through your refrigerator and pantry shelves, and note what you need and what you still have plenty of. Add to the list any sale-priced specials you may not need this week, but which you will be needing before they come on sale again.

The last thing to do before going grocery shopping is to eat a good breakfast or lunch. Countless studies have shown that hungry shoppers are impulse shoppers. Shop for food when you're hungry and you'll spend 25 to 30 percent more than you intended to buy.

Many people are not aware of one of the best shopping sources to buy high-quality kitchen utensils at prices that are generally much lower than at so-called kitchenware boutiques. I am talking about the restaurant-supply companies which provide cookware to professional chefs. Most "civilians" do not know that they can walk right in off the street into a restaurant-supply store and buy stainless-steel spoons, bowls, and kettles. Of course, the sizes will be large, but you'll find you can't beat the quality.

"Restaurant Equipment and Supplies" is the heading in my Yellow Pages. One of the things I recommend you pick up from such a store is a baker's brush. They are available in several widths. I find they're unbeatable for greasing the frying pan when I'm cooking a lot of things, such as pancakes or crepes. Have a bowl or jar of oil handy to dip the brush into. One swipe with the brush on the pan puts down the thin film of oil that you need. It's far better to apply a little oil more often than to have an excess of oil, smoking and burning around the edges of the frying pan.

A good way to identify an efficient cook is by how little food he or she has to throw away. It does you no good to be a wise shopper and save 10 cents on a head of lettuce if that lettuce wilts in your refrigerator before you can use it up.

So here are some tips on how to be a good greenskeeper. When you bring a head of lettuce home from the market, before you put it away in the refrigerator, separate it into individual leaves and wash them thoroughly in cold, running water. Alternate dried leaves of lettuce between sheets of paper toweling, and store the entire bundle in a clear plastic bag, closed with a twist tie, in your refrigerator's vegetable keeper. It will last twice as long without wilting.

When you bring home a full stalk of celery, trim off the leafy tops, but for goodness' sake, don't throw them away. Store them in a plastic container in your freezer. The next time you make soups or stews, add celery tops. After several minutes of simmering, nobody will ever know they had been frozen.

The main stalks of celery should be separated and washed clean. Store them in a large, tall jar or plastic container that you have filled with water. Keep it capped, and celery will stay crisp and fresh for up to two weeks. Treat carrots the same way. A recycled cardboard milk carton is another handy container to keep these low-calorie snacks handy and ready to crunch.

I must confess a fondness for celery stalks with peanut butter spread into the groove down the center. The celery keeps the peanut butter from sticking to the roof of your mouth.

You can keep fresh parsley for two to three weeks by following this method: pack parsley sprigs into a glass jar and sprinkle with salt, 1 teaspoon of salt to 1 cup of parsley. Cover jar and shake to distribute salt evenly, then add cold water to fill jar. Shake again and store in refrigerator. When you need parsley, rinse off brine before using.

To chop parsley very finely, use scissors instead of a knife. Put parsley into a small glass tumber. Then snip with repeated chops of scissors while inside the glass.

To store radishes, first trim off the tops. Then store in a glass jar of water to which you have added sugar, honey, or even corn syrup, 1/2 teaspoon to 1 teaspoon for every 2 cups of water. The number of calories added is insignificant.

How often do you find a recipe calling for one or two tablespoonfuls of diced onion? Unless you keep a good supply of very tiny onions on hand, you're like me and you end up with half to three-quarters of an onion left over. Don't just wrap it up in plastic wrap and put it back into your refrigerator; it will go weird. Dice the entire onion and store the unused portion in a glass jar, plastic bag, or container in your freezer. You can not only put it into soups or stews, but you can also sauté frozen, chopped onion just as if it were fresh. If you don't think this works, check the frozen vegetable section at your supermarket. You'll find chopped, frozen onions there now, selling for about three to four times the cost of doing it yourself.

You can save canned tomato paste the same way. When the recipe calls for one or two tablespoonfuls, don't throw away the remaining two-thirds of a can. Put the balance in a little plastic container in your freezer. The next time you need a little more, just scoop out a tablespoonful or two of frozen tomato paste, right into your saucepan or frying pan.

When you have one or two slices of tomato left over from making B.L.T. sandwiches, save the remains in your freezer. A few chunks of frozen tomato, when added to the can or jar of commercial spaghetti sauce you're heating up, will fool your friends into thinking you've been slaving all day over a hot saucepan.

Leftover red and green bell peppers can also be

frozen. As a matter of fact, the tomato is the vegetable that suffers most from freezing, but when used in sauces or stews, you'll hardly notice the difference. Lettuce and cabbage freeze very poorly, indeed. But a quick trick when you're cooking cabbage rolls is to separate the cabbage leaves, stack them on paper towels, put them in a pan and freeze them for an hour or two. When you take them out and they thaw, they'll be wilted and pliable for wrapping around your favorite meat-and-tomato mixture, to turn into classic Hungarian or Ukrainian cabbage rolls.

All fresh fruit, but particularly bananas, peaches, pears, and nectarines will ripen more quickly when placed in a plastic bag, sealed, at room temperature for 24 to 36 hours. The fruit releases natural gases which assist the ripening process. Adding a banana to a bag of ripening avocados will help them ripen faster than if the avocados were in the bag by themselves.

If your bananas are in danger of becoming too ripe, peel them, put banana chunks into a blender or food processor with one teaspoonful of lemon juice or lime juice per banana, and zap them into a pulp. This will keep in the refrigerator for up to one week; freezing is better. Scoop out as much as you need. It thaws out fast for use in banana-loaf bread or banana pancakes.

You can make delicious frozen-banana treats by whipping together 4 or 5 mashed bananas, 1½ tablespoons lemon juice, 3 or 4 tablespoons of fructose, honey, or cornsyrup and 1/2 cup of skim milk. Whirl or process the mixture thoroughly, and freeze in plastic molds with sticks. They are refreshing and nutritious snacks.

Nothing ruins the taste of a good banana-nut loaf faster than rancid nuts. You would be surprised at how quickly nuts go rancid, especially those high in oil, such as walnuts, pecans, cashews, almonds, and Macadamia nuts. They will keep much better when stored in a glass jar with a good sealing lid, in the freezer. You'll also find that even unshelled nuts can be frozen. After the Christmas holidays have passed, pour the remnants of your bowlfuls of Brazil nuts, walnuts, and hazel nuts into a bag and place it in your freezer. Frozen nuts in the shell are easier to crack than fresh ones are.

Frozen roasts of beef or veal do not have to be thawed before roasting. Preheat the oven to 400^0 and roast the frozen beef or veal at this higher temperature for the first half-hour. After 30 minutes, reduce the heat to 325^0 and continue roasting as normal. Searing at 400^0 locks the juices into the meat; these would be lost if you thawed it first. And never pre-salt a roast. You can rub on garlic, pepper, and herbs before it goes into the oven, but keep the salt away until roasting is done.

Roasting frozen pork, however, is never recommended. Although today's modern meat-handling methods and inspection processes have greatly reduced the chances of pork being infected with trichinosis and other parasite-related disorders, it is still very important that pork be thoroughly cooked. The center of the roast must reach a meat thermometer reading of no lower than 175^0. I personally feel safer if my pork is slightly overcooked.

One product which does not seem to enjoy being frozen is coffee. Whole coffee beans may be stored longer than ground coffee, which has a shelf-life of only one week, even when kept in the refrigerator. To get the maximum life from coffee, store whole beans in a tightly sealed glass jar in the refrigerator, and grind only as much as you use at any one time.

But be careful how you store coffee. If you wash the storage jar in lemon-scented dishwashing liquid, make certain the jar is thoroughly rinsed and aired out before storing coffee beans inside. If you are not careful, you could end up with a very strange lemon-flavored coffee.

Coffee, by the way, is very good at spreading its aromas in the environment. That is why a bowlful of coffee grounds makes a good deodorizer or air freshener.

Just for the Health of It

"Go ahead line eight."

"Is it true that you should store makeup in the refrigerator, to keep it from going bad?"

"I can give you a very firm, definite answer to that question. Yes, no, or maybe. Yes you should store makeup in the fridge, but no, the reason is not to keep it from going bad, in the sense you probably mean."

I went on to explain the reason why makeup should be kept refrigerated. It is to maintain cleanliness.

Over the years I have interviewed numerous dermatologists and cosmetologists. Seldom do the two professions see eye to eye. But one factor on which they do seem to find common ground is the importance of cleanliness in skin care.

Your skin is a constant breeding ground for bacteria. This is especially true around the eyes, nose, mouth, and ears, the areas where women apply most makeup. Whatever you use to apply makeup can pick up bacteria when it makes contact with the skin.

Lipsticks, mascara brushes, sponges, powder pads, lipstick brushes, eyebrow pencils, your fingers, go from the makeup container to your skin, and then they return to the makeup container. As they return, they carry bacteria with them. The bacteria grow in the makeup container, waiting for you to apply it again tomorrow.

One way to avoid transferring bacteria into makeup containers is to use disposable applicators; cotton balls and cotton-tipped swabs. Another way is to keep applicators as clean as possible. Disinfect sponges at least once a week. Never let anyone else use your lipstick or powder puff.

Refrigeration is another good way to reduce bacteria. Any makeup you use only occasionally or seasonally should be stored in the refrigerator. As most makeup should only be applied at room temperature, this is impractical for the liquids and creams you use every day. Nail polish can be kept in the fridge all the time. This is especially important during hot summer months. Colors stay true and nail polish maintains its texture better when it is kept cool.

Did you know that where you apply your makeup can be as important as how you apply it? My wife, Ramona Beauchamp, an expert in modeling, makeup, and personal care, asked me to pass along this tip: beware of applying your daytime makeup in the bathroom.

Many bathrooms allow no natural light in. The light bulbs give off light that may be a significantly different color temperature than natural daylight. Therefore, the way your makeup looks in your bathroom may be vastly different from the way it actually appears when you step out into the daylight. Have you ever seen a woman with so much makeup on she almost looked like a clown, with bright-red rouge circles on her cheeks? Chances are, she looked fine in her bathroom mirror at home.

To make sure you don't apply too much daytime makeup, put it on in natural daylight. A dressing table

beside a window is the best solution if your bedroom
does not let the sun shine in.

If this is not possible, consult a makeup expert, or
a professional lighting dealer to obtain lighting fixtures

that most closely approximate the color temperature of natural light.

Makeup applicators are not the only places where we must be careful to avoid a build-up of bacteria. If you use long-lasting razor blades, or if you keep disposable razors longer than a week, you should use a disinfectant on them. Once a week, clean the blades with rubbing alcohol, to prevent bacteria from building up.

Old prescriptions can be even more dangerous than old cosmetics. If you ever discover leftover prescription medications that are no longer being used, destroy them. Be careful not to throw them away where children might pick them up. Old antibiotics are particularly dangerous. They can deteriorate or their strength can change. If your doctor should issue a prescription for medicine you may already have, throw away the old stuff and get new, fresh medicine, especially if the stored medication is more than six months old.

An Editorial

"Sorry, line nine. This chapter is reserved for a few personal comments."

I want to discuss some fiction and facts about nutrition and health. In addition to the truths and falsehoods, there are also a lot of maybes.

In the past decade alone, some giant steps have been taken in the fields of nutrition and health research. New discoveries have shown that some of our old practices and habits have been detrimental to our personal health. But when we are dealing with things that mom and dad said were OK, as did their parents and their grandparents, it can be painfully hard to change our ways.

You probably already know that I feel egg yolks are not food we should be eating. Saturated animal and vegetable fats are the greatest contributors to dangerous levels of cholesterol in our arteries. And it pains me to say that the poor old cackleberry, your delicious breakfast egg, is the single biggest culprit in our diet. It is generally accepted by the majority of nutritionists and cardiovascular experts that one whole egg per week provides as much low-density cholesterol as the human body can tolerate.

Before you start to question whether life is still worth living, let me inform you that, fortunately, there are now several substitutes available on the market that can successfully be used as replacements for eggs and other animal fats. My hat is off to the Fleishman Corporation for the production of an egg substitute called Egg Beaters. They are made primarily from egg whites, with some corn oil and other ingredients. They are not only delicious when scrambled or whipped into omelets or soufflés, but they also can be baked into custards and used in recipes equally as well as the original that comes straight from the hen.

According to some of the foremost experts on fats and oils, the best substitute for butter now available in both Canada and the U.S. is a margarine called Becel. It is suitable for low-cholesterol diets.

The Canadian Heart Foundation and Health and Welfare Canada recommend using vegetable oils which contain a polyunsaturated fatty acid called linoleic acid. Safflower oil and grape-seed oil contain the highest concentration, followed by corn oil, soya oil, peanut oil, and, at the low end of the scale, olive oil.

Many of us have been told, by parents and others, that honey is better for you than refined, granulated sugar, because honey is "more natural." I have had some rather interesting discussions with honey producers, who get annoyed at some of the things I say on the radio about honey. But the facts I give you are not my fabrications. They come from nutrition experts from leading universities. They lead to the conclusion that honey is not better for you than sugar. Biochemically, the human system sees them as nearly identical, although there is a higher percentage of fructose in honey. It is also higher in calories than granulated sugar. Liquid sugar syrups, such as pancake syrup, are nearly equal in calorie content to honey.

Most important, the medical profession has advised against feeding honey to any child under age two. The reason is that honey is a potential carrier for dormant spores of colostridium botulinum, one of the deadliest bacteria known to mankind.

Deaths have occurred in Canada and the U.S. to infants who were given honey at too early an age. Your pediatrician can confirm that administering honey as a soother to children under age two is unwise.

On the positive side, I love the flavor of honey, and I find it a superior sweetener to most forms of sugar. I use it at home regularly, especially for the unique flavor it gives to hot cocoa drinks. But I would never give it to my children or grandchildren, knowing the potential dangers.

As far as honey being more natural than sugar is concerned, I say "rubbish!" The bee refines honey through its system many more times than man does when he refines the juice of the sugar cane or sugar beet. Man simply extracts the water and puts the concentrated sugar through a centrifuge to aid in crystalization. Is evaporation less natural than a concentrated extract from the digestive system of an insect?

I have to chuckle at the notion that brown sugar is nutritionally superior to white sugar. Brown sugar is nothing more than white sugar to which a tiny amount of molasses has been added, to give it a different texture and color. In order to get enough of the trace minerals to make a difference to your diet, you would have to eat five or six pounds of straight molasses per day. Eat brown sugar if you like the way it tastes, but thinking brown sugar is better for you than white sugar is a mistake.

Fiber has become the most popular nutritional buzzword of the decade. There is no questioning that fiber is important. There is fiber in the majority of the fruits and vegetables we consume. It is in whole grains, legumes, lentils, peas, beans, etc. Some have more fiber than others. It has been shown that people who eat a high-fiber diet tend to have fewer problems than others do with overweight, heart disease, and cancer of the lower intestine. Today, it is nearly impossible to find a breakfast-cereal package that is not covered with information about fiber. Many cereals have added wheat or oat bran.

It should be noted that certain medical conditions result in a low tolerance for fiber. Too much fiber in the diet can also interfere with the body's ability to absorb such essential minerals as iron, calcium, and zinc.

One of the most exciting pieces of information to come along in the world of fibers deals with oat bran. Some of the latest studies show that oat bran is more effective than any other fiber at reducing blood-serum cholesterol levels, according to some laboratory experiments. Some health professionals suspect that oat bran may be one of the best overall fiber foods we can include in our daily diets. One to two tablespoonfuls per day of dietary oat bran seems to be the normal requirement.

It would be wonderful if eating more fiber would work even better at flushing cholesterol out of our systems faster; but the body does not work that way. Talk to your doctor if you are concerned about your cholesterol count. And try to keep your consumption of bacon, eggs, butter, cream, and fatty meats down to a minimum.

Some recent information regarding fish oils gives us even more hope for the future of our arteries. I recommend the book, "Fats and Oils, the Complete Guide to Fats and Oils in Health and Nutrition" by a biochemist, Udo Erasmus. After spending many years researching low- and high-density cholesterol, he has revealed the beneficial properties of a certain oil found in fatty fish, particularly salmon, mackerel, trout, and eel.

Many people who have for years enjoyed delicious fresh baked bread, rolls, and buns may be shocked to learn that possibly as much as 60 percent of our population may be allergic to wheat. Wheat intolerance can be mild or severe, and symptoms can range from small headaches and sinus discomfort to rashes, diarrhea, breathing difficulties, and even loss of consciousness. If you have any doubts about what happens to you when you eat wheat-based products, consult your physician about it. It may be a good idea for your doctor to recommend an allergy specialist. It is profoundly difficult these days to avoid coming into contact with wheat-based products.

Try reading the labels of the food products you find on the shelves of your supermarket. Keep track of the number of products that contain wheat, eggs, saturated fats, preservatives such as sodium nitrite and sodium nitrate. Monosodium glutimate is still used by major soup producers and food processors. It is hard to avoid consuming these things.

Our society has at its disposal the greatest abundance of nutritional information ever assembled. Yet all too many people ignore the facts, preferring to believe the advertising they see and hear. Concern about cholesterol caused by so-called junk foods may be a thing of the past if what one now hears about Proctor and Gamble's new product, sucrose polyester, turns out to be true. This potential substitute for fats and oils supposedly produces the same results in deep frying and cooking as do today's oils and saturated fats, but it cannot be absored by the human body.

Already available to today's consumers are numerous substitutes for high-fat, high-calorie or allergy-causing foods. In addition to the egg and butter substitutes are oat flour, corn flour, millet flour, rice flour, barley flour, soya flour, and chick-pea flour, all of which can replace wheat flour. People who should not eat yeasts can enjoy baked goods made with baking soda.

Cutting down on fatty meats once meant either fish, chicken, or that semi-food known as tuna casserole. But in the past ten years, the turkey industry has brought us some marvelous alternatives. Available in increasing locations is a wide range of products made from turkey. They include breakfast and dinner sausages, cold cuts, and steaks and cutlets which can be prepared the same way as traditionally delicious schnitzel and veal parmesan. I enjoy products from a company on the West Coast of Canada that makes pastrami, garlic rings, hams, salami, pepperoni, and more, from turkey. They contain no additives or preservatives, are 50 to 70 percent lower in fat content than their conventional meat counterparts, and are 100 percent as delicious. If you are sensitive to M.S.G. or sodium nitrites, check to make sure the turkey products you buy contain no such additives.

Companies that deal in high volumes of products find such preservatives a necessity in increasing the shelf life of their foods.

There is also some very good news for those of us who enjoy the flavor of a good beef roast or steak. According to recent Canadian government information, the cholesterol content of beef may have been erroneously measured from 20 to 40 percent higher than it actually is. This still does not say that the crackling on the roast or the fatty marbling in the steak is good for you. Pretend it tastes as bad as it is bad for you. Trim off excess fat from beef, pork, lamb, and chicken and other poultry.

I appreciate that, with all the information now available to us, much of it is confusing and some of it is even contradictory. My recommendation is moderation in all things, including moderation.

Edging my way further out onto my limb, I gaze into my crystal ball and I visualize life on earth in 2037, 50 years from now. Assuming this old planet hasn't been destroyed in the meantime, life will be changed in several ways. Smoking will have been totally eliminated. Remember, nobody smoked in Europe until Sir Walter Raleigh brought tobacco back from North America, less than 400 years ago.

Cholesterol intake will be controlled in 2037. People will enjoy fun in the sun but nobody will have, or want to have a tan. Exercise will have increased our lifespans, our sex lives will be fantastic, and we will all have the body we desire. And people who write problem-solving books will all be out of business.

You can take this prediction to heart, or take it with a grain of salt. And you know what too much salt can do to your blood pressure!

Good luck, take care, and have a good day.

Good day!

How-to Guide

A to Z Guide to Stain Removal, Household Hints, and Personal Care

Adhesive Tape Remove tape residue from skin using cooking oil or peanut butter. On hard surfaces such as glass, use solvent, rubbing alcohol, or paint thinner.

Alcohol Remove white rings and stains on wooden furniture caused by alcoholic beverages or other liquids as well as condensation marks caused by glasses or cups. See *Furniture*.

Rubbing alcohol is also good for removing shoepolish (liquid and paste); ink, crayon marks from walls, and lipstick marks from hard surfaces and fabrics.

Alligator Skin Clean reptile leather with a mild solution of 1 teaspoon of liquid dishwashing soap to 1 pint of water. Apply with a soft, dampened cloth, do not soak, and always rub in the direction of the scales. Shoe and luggage dealers sell commercial cleaners.

Aphids Use insecticidal soap to kill aphids on plants. I recommend Safer's products in Canada. Or make a mild solution of water and detergent, and spray onto plants.

Apple Juice Stain See *Fruit Juice Stain*

Arborite Clean table and countertops with sudsy, lukewarm water. Apply any paste-type floorwax, and buff to a shine.

Avocado Stain Carefully scrape off solid matter. Rinse washable fabrics in cold water. Work in liquid dishwashing detergent with fingers. Rinse in cold water.

On carpets, scrape up solid matter. Flush with soda water (bottled or mix 1 tablespoon baking soda with 1 pint water). Make a pad of cloth 2 to 3 inches thick. Old white towels work best. Rinse them out in cold water, then wring them until barely damp. Place over stain and tamp down with foot. Let them absorb liquid from carpet. If any stain remains, apply shaving foam to area, flush with soda water, and use towel pack to absorb liquid.

Ballpoint Pen Ink Stain Remove from skin with rubbing alcohol. On fabric, first put a cloth on underside to prevent stain from spreading. Treat ink with rubbing alcohol or cleaning solvent. Or wash blue and black inks in a mixture of vinegar and liquid detergent. Use sudsy ammonia on red or brown inks.

Banana Stain Same as *Avocado.*

Bathtub Stain Remove blue-green scale caused by dripping water with a slush of salt and vinegar. Rub on with soft cloth. Rinse with lots of cold water.

Bee Spots On windows and painted surfaces: if fresh, wipe as soon as possible with liquid dishwashing detergent and lukewarm water. If dry, scrape off with plastic or wooden scraper. Wash with soft cloth and warm, sudsy water.

Beer Spill On Carpet Blot up liquid. Flush with soda water. Absorb with thick pad of towels tamped onto area.

Beet Stain Flush with cold water. Work liquid detergent into stain. Use enzyme pre-treat before laundering. On washable whites, rub borax onto stain and work in solution of 1 tablespoon baking soda and 1 tablespoon

liquid detergent to 1 pint water.

Binoculars Clean lenses with window cleaner or mixture of 1 teaspoon vinegar to 1 cup water. Apply with soft, lint-free cloth. Clean binocular body with weak solution of liquid detergent and baking soda with lukewarm water. Apply with soft, clean cloth.

Bird Droppings Remove as soon as possible from car, as high acid content can damage paint. Flush with solution of baking soda and cold water. If you live in a high-risk seagull zone, carry a spray bottle of water and baking soda in your car.

Blinds, Venetian Mix solution of 1 quart water, 3 tablespoons vinegar, and 2 teaspoons liquid detergent. Wipe blinds with damp cloth. Heavily soiled blinds may be washed in bathtub. Half fill tub with lukewarm water, 1 cup liquid detergent, and ½ cup vinegar. Swish blinds in tub, rinse with shower, and hang from shower curtain rod.

Blood Stain   On washable fabrics, dampen with cold water and sprinkle with meat tenderizer (or enzyme pre-soak). Repeat process with fresh tenderizer or pre-soak on heavily stained areas. Wash in sudsy, lukewarm water.

On nonwashables, dampen stain with cold water, sprinkle with table salt, brush off, dampen again, sprinkle with meat tenderizer, allow to dry, blot with clean, damp cloth. If any stain remains, have garment dry-cleaned.

On mattresses, lean mattress against a wall, on its side. Dampen stain with cold water and sprinkle with meat tenderizer. Leave on 1 hour, then wipe with damp cloth, moistened with water and disinfectant. Lay mattress back down and apply pack of towels to absorb moisture. If all else fails, use 1 part hydrogen peroxide to 4 parts water. But be warned, it will bleach colors.

Blueberry Stain Flush thoroughly with cold water. Work in baking soda and liquid detergent. Soak in enzyme pre-treat before laundering.

Blue Jeans See *Grease*

Books   Treat grease stains on pages by dusting with cornstarch to absorb grease, then brush off.

To clean leather covers, dampen cloth with saddle soap and lukewarm water. Rub in and dry immediately with soft, clean cloth.

Brass Clean with toothpaste on an old toothbrush, or scrub with slush of salt and vinegar. Commercial brass cleaners are most effective.

Burns Clip out burned carpet fibers with manicure scissors. Trim fresh fibers from unseen area of carpet (under baseboard or furniture) and glue into spot with rubber cement.

Carbon Paper Stain On washable fabrics, apply rubbing alcohol with a cotton ball. On synthetics, use a powder spray cleaner such as Texize K2r.

Cameras Same as *Binoculars*

Carpets, Liquid Stains If you have a shop/vac or a vacuum cleaner designed to vacuum up liquids, you may use it instead of the method of blotting with a pad of towels described elsewhere in this book. Flush the stained area with the appropriate liquid and simultaneously vacuum the saturated area. When the stain is washed out, use a dry towel to blot up remaining moisture. Refer to the various treatments for specific carpet stains in this appendix.

If you do not wish to treat carpet stains yourself, keep the stain from drying out before the professional carpet cleaner arrives. Dampen water soluble stains with water. For grease or oil stains, or on carpets that cannot be treated with water, cover stain with plastic to prevent air from drying the stain.

If you are taking a stained rug to be cleaned, roll it in plastic to prevent the stain from being transferred to a clean area.

Ceramic Tiles Clean with baking soda and lukewarm water, or a non-abrasive commercial product.

Chamois (Chammy) To soften this leather, soak in a solution of 1 quart lukewarm water to 1 teaspoon olive oil or vegetable oil. Soak for 1 hour, wringing out several times during the hour.

Chandeliers Clean crystal chandeliers with window cleaner or a solution of water and vinegar, applied with a soft cloth to individual pieces. If chandelier can be removed in its entirety and *no electrical connections are involved,* immerse it in a bathtub filled with a solution of lukewarm water and liquid automatic-dishwasher detergent. Use shower to rinse.

Cherry Stain Same as *Blueberry Stain*

China, Bone Never wash fine china in electric dishwasher, nor use abrasive cleaners or scrapers. Wash with mild detergent and lukewarm water. Rinse each piece individually and wipe dry with soft, clean, lint-free towel.

Chocolate Stain Scrape off solids with spatula or back of knife. Stretch washable fabric over mixing bowl, with stain centered over bowl. Work liquid dishwashing soap or sudsy ammonia into stain. Pour hot water from a height of two to three feet through the stain. Repeat if necessary.

Cleaning Solvent A universally accepted cleaning solution usually produced by the petrochemical industry as a byproduct of gasoline production. Normally sold as a nonflammable cleaning solution through service stations and hardware stores. Sometimes available in department stores and supermarkets in the automotive or household cleaning department.

Cocoa, Dry Powder Vacuum powder as soon as possible from fabric or carpet. If residue remains, rinse with cold water and work in liquid detergent. Rinse.

Cocoa, Hot Chocolate With Milk On carpet, flush with soda water and blot up liquid with thick pad of damp cloths. Remove residue with carpet shampoo or shaving foam. Work from outside inwards. Wipe gently with cloth dampened in cool water. Wring out thick pad of cloths and re-apply, tamping down with foot. Allow to draw moisture up from fibers.

On fabric, use sudsy ammonia and water. Or mix lukewarm water and liquid detergent with a drop or two of household ammonia. Flush with water.

Coffee Stain On washable fabrics, blot up liquid, then flush with a solution of 4 parts water to 1 part white vinegar. Add liquid detergent or mild hand soap, working it in with fingers. Flush with lukewarm water. If stain persists, white fabrics may be treated with a solution of 1 part hydrogen peroxide to six parts of water. Soak 1 to 2 hours.

Coffee stains on silks, woolens, or other dry-cleanable garments should be treated by flushing area with cool water and taking garment to your professional dry cleaner.

Treat coffee stains on carpets by blotting up as much coffee as possible, then mix 1 tablespoon of liquid detergent with 1/3 cup white vinegar and 2/3 cup water. Apply the solution, blot the carpet, and gently brush the pile, working from outside inwards to avoid spreading stain. Then apply thick pad of towels, tamp down, and allow to draw remaining moisture out.

Coffee Maker Cleaning and Descaling Fill automatic coffee maker with water. Add 1 tablespoon of baking soda to 10. cups of water, and run coffee maker through full cycle.

Copper If no commercial copper cleaner is available, clean with toothpaste on an old toothbrush. Or scrub with a slush of salt and vinegar.

Cork Boards and Paneling If removable, sprinkle cork boards with cornstarch to absorb grease and dirt. Vacuum, using upholstery brush. Vacuum nonremovable cork paneling with upholstery brush and clean stubborn spots with commercial cleaning dough, available from paneling or wallpaper dealers.

Crayon Marks Remove from painted walls using warm (not hot) iron. Cover mark with dry paper towel and apply warm iron for a few moments. Crayon wax will melt and paper towel will absorb it. Remove residue from latex-painted walls with paint thinner on a soft cloth. On oil-based paint, use a small amount of rubbing alcohol on a soft cloth, and rub very gently. On washable wallpaper, clean with rubbing alcohol on a damp cloth. On non-washable wallpaper, rub very gently with a dry, soap-filled, steel-wool pad.

Remove crayon marks from vinyl or plastic with rubbing alcohol or liquid silver polish, or other liquid (not paste) metal polish.

Creosote Remove from washable fabric using safe cleaning solvent such as those available at a service station or hardware store. Apply with clean, soft cloth. Remember to place another cloth behind stain to avoid transfer to other parts of garment. Treat stain thoroughly with

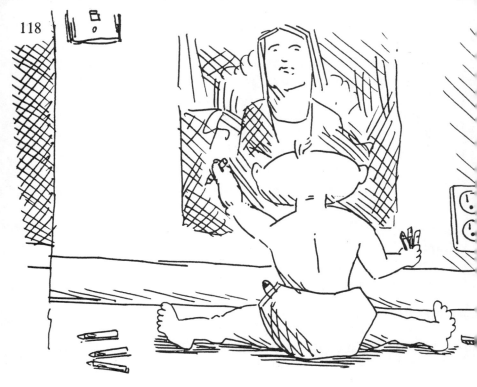

cleaning solvent, then blot with clean, dry cloth. If a dark smudge remains, apply straight liquid detergent, work in with fingers, and flush with lukewarm water.

On dry-cleanable fabrics, remove any excess creosote as soon as possible; follow with solvent on a soft cloth. Have dry cleaner treat if any stain remains.

Crystal Bowls and Vases Clean with sudsy ammonia and water, or vinegar and water. Liquid window cleaner also is effective.

Crystal Decanters Clean inside with solution of 5 parts water to 1 part sudsy ammonia. Add 1 tablespoon of uncooked rice (not instant type). Stopper decanter, grasp firmly (rubber gloves help prevent slippage), and shake violently. Rice will work as an abrasive to scrub inside clean. If stain is milky residue, fill decanter with warm water and baking soda, allow to soak 24 hours, then add rice and shake.

Crystal Stemware Wash in electric dishwasher only by themselves, never with other soiled items. Use liquid automatic-dishwashing detergent, not powder. Do not allow to go through drying cycle. Dry by hand, regardless of dishwasher manufacturer's recommendations.

Curry Gravy Stain To clean from washable fabric, first allow to dry, and scrape off solids. Isolate the remaining stain and flush with cold water. Rub liquid detergent in with fingers, and add warmer water. Continue treatment with more detergent and increasingly warmer water. On white or colorfast garments, add 1 part water to 4 parts vinegar and use instead of detergent.

On carpets, scrape up solids and flush with soda water. Blot up with thick pad of damp towels. Make a foam by beating 1 teaspoon liquid detergent and 1/2 teaspoon borax into 1 cup of water. Beat with wire whip into a foam. Apply to stain and blot up. Re-apply and blot until color of stain is gone. Then flush with soda water and apply blotting pack. Leave pack on 2 hours, then rinse it out, wring it out, and re-apply.

Remove curry stains from plastic bowls or containers with smoker's toothpaste, applied with an old toothbrush. Add lukewarm water to the toothpaste.

Dandelion Yellow stains on children's clothing. On white and colorfast fabrics, apply toothpaste to stain, add lukewarm water, and work in with fingers. Or use liquid detergent mixed with vinegar. For sensitive colored fabrics, soak in enzyme pre-treat before laundering.

Dents In Wooden Furniture Place a wet cloth over dent and apply a hot iron. The steam will cause the wood to expand, and raise dent. Not recommended on lacquered or varnished surfaces.

Diamond Jewelry Clean with toothpaste and lukewarm water, applied with a soft bristle brush. Or rinse in lukewarm water and window-cleaning solution. Polish with a soft cloth or chamois.

Diapers Soak cloth diapers in a solution of borax and water for one half-hour before laundering.

Diaper Stain On Carpet See *Urine*

Dishes, China (Ordinary) For best results in washing everyday dishes, add a few drops of vinegar to water in sink or tub, along with detergent. In electric dishwasher, rinse all dishes before loading (regardless of manufacturer's claims). Use no vinegar in electric dishwasher. Check reservoir of drying agent every month or so, and refill when empty. Even in soft-water areas, drying agent does result in cleaner dishes and fewer spots.

Dishes, Plastic If difficult stains remain after dishwashing, scrub with toothpaste on an old brush. Rinse with lukewarm water.

Dye Stain Blot up fresh spots. Add no water. Place old towel behind stain to prevent transfer. Apply rubbing alcohol with cotton ball or spray with hairspray. Allow to penetrate 30 seconds, then blot up. Use same procedure for dye stain on carpet. Repeat if necessary. Never launder washable fabrics before pre-treating stain, or any residual dye will be set permanently.

Egg Stain, White or Yolk On washable fabrics, flush area with cold water. Apply sudsy ammonia. Flush and repeat two or three times until all material is removed. Never use hot water, as it will cook the egg into the fibers.

On nonwashables, isolate the stain and treat with cold water and mild hand soap only.

On carpets, blot up as much material as possible. Then treat area with cold water and shaving foam or carpet shampoo. Wipe up excess, then apply thick pad of damp, clean towels, tamped down with foot. Allow pad to sit on stain up to 2 hours, to absorb liquid from fibers.

Electric Frying Pans Grease builds up underneath exterior. Use commercial cleaner or scrub with toothpaste mixed with cleaning solvent applied with an old toothbrush. Rinse and dry thoroughly. Never immerse in water. Follow manufacturer's instructions to clean inside pan.

Eyeglasses See *Binoculars*

Fat Stains Butter, margarine, animal fats, cooking oil, or shortening on washable or nonwashable fabrics may be treated with cornstarch. Sprinkle onto spot, pat in with hand to blot oil. Repeat if necessary. Brush off cornstarch. Treat remaining stain on washable fabrics with liquid detergent to which a few drops of cleaning solvent have been added. Work in with fingers. Rinse with lukewarm water. Repeat if necessary.

On nonwashable fabrics, place an old towel behind the stain to prevent its transfer to remaining garment. Apply cleaning solvent with a clean, soft cloth. Always work stain from outside toward center to avoid spreading. If any stain remains, have garment dry-cleaned.

On carpets, scrape or blot up excess. Test a small, unseen area of carpet to determine whether nonflammable dry-cleaning solvent is safe prior to treating stain. Blot dry.

Felt Marker Ink Back stain on fabric with an old towel to prevent transfer. Try cleaning red or brown ink with liquid dishwashing soap and sudsy ammonia. On blue or black ink, use solution of 2/3 cup water and 1/3 cup vinegar mixed with 1 tablespoon detergent.

On hard surfaces such as arborite or appliances, use rubbing alcohol on a soft, clean cloth, followed by rinsing immediately with warm, sudsy water. Wipe dry.

On unfinished wood, sand with sandpaper.

On varnished furniture, mix 4 parts cooking oil to 1 part rubbing alcohol. Apply with clean, soft cloth to a small area at a time. Try to avoid contact with unstained area. Wipe up immediately with a clean cloth. Or use sudsy ammonia on a clean cloth and dry area immediately. See also *Furniture*

Fireplace Clean the interior masonry using a stiff bristle brush and muriatic acid. Wear goggles, gloves, and protective clothing. You may also use trisodium phosphate, available from hardware stores. Follow instructions carefully.

Clean exterior marble by washing with a solution of vinegar and water. Dry thoroughly. Use a paste of baking soda and water, or jeweler's rouge, for difficult stains. Polish marble fireplace or table tops with hard floor wax, never paste or liquids.

Flower Pollen Stain First, vacuum up powder, then treat as a solid fruit stain. See *Fruit Stain, Solid*

Fly Specks See *Bee Spots*

Food Coloring See *Dye*

Fruit Juice Stain On washable fabrics, soak in cold water. If necessary, work in liquid soap and rinse. If any stain remains, work in more soap mixed with vinegar and lukewarm water, and rinse.

On dry-cleanable fabrics, isolate stain area, sponge with cold water to which a few drops of liquid dishwashing soap have been added. Blot dry, then rinse.

On carpets, flush with soda water (either bottled or a mix of 1 tablespoon baking soda to 1 pint water), then blot with thick pad of damp cloths. Apply shaving foam or carpet shampoo and work into fibers gently. Flush with soda water again and blot up liquid. Wring out pad of cloths, re-apply, and leave on 1 to 2 hours, to draw up remaining liquid. On stains such as raspberry or grape juice, where there is a high color content, repeat the process several times.

Fruit Stain, Solids On washable fabrics, allow stain to dry, then scrape off residue. Work liquid dishwashing soap into remaining stain with fingers. Flush with cool water. If stubborn stain persists, treat with mixture of 2/3 cup water, 1/3 cup vinegar, and 1 tablespoon liquid soap. Rinse with cool water.

On dry-cleanable fabrics, remove excess fruit solids. Isolate stain and sponge with mixture of 1 part rubbing alcohol to 2 parts cold water. Mop up excess with a clean, dry cloth.

On carpets, scrape up solid material. Flush with soda water. Soak up with thick pad of damp cloths. Apply shaving foam or carpet shampoo, work in, and flush with soda water. If any color remains, whisk together foam made from 1 cup water, 2 teaspoons liquid detergent, and 1 teaspoon rubbing alcohol. Apply with clean cloth, rub in, blot up, and repeat if necessary. Finally, apply damp pad of cloths to spot, tamp down with foot, and allow to stand 1 to 2 hours.

Fruit Stain On Dishes Scrub with toothpaste (smoker's or regular) and lukewarm water, applied with an old toothbrush.

Furniture, Cleaning and Restoring Here is the best homemade furniture stain remover and furniture restorer that you could possibly find. It is the proven formula of one of Canada's best furniture finishers who has done several shows with me over the years, Mr. Bernie Kneller of Surrey, B.C., now retired. It cleans and polishes even the toughest stain.

Bernie's Furniture Restorer
2 parts cooking oil
2 parts turpentine
1 part vinegar
½ part rubbing alcohol

Use as a standard wooden furniture cleaner and restorer. Shake well before using and apply with soft cloth. In extreme cases, use triple 0 steel wool applied gently to surface with pressure from the weight of your hand. Remove excess with clean, soft cloth.

Glue, Krazy and Others Some brands can be removed only by using solvent made by glue manufacturer. Others will dissolve with acetone. *Caution:* never use acetone on acetate fabrics. Never buy glue without buying solvent. Always wear gloves, avoid contact with skin, and follow manufacturer's instructions.

Gold Chains Wash in a bowl of warm water and liquid detergent. Brush with an old toothbrush if necessary. Rinse, dry, and polish with chamois or soft, lint-free cloth.

Gold Leaf Make a solution from 10 parts water to 1 part

ammonia. Apply gently with a soft, clean cloth.

Gravy See *Fat*

Grease Scrape up excess grease, then follow the procedure for *Fat.*

Grease, Petrochemical If working on machinery outdoors, pack grease spot on jeans with dirt or sand to soak up excess and prevent spreading. Repeat as necessary. Pre-treat with commercial product, or use this easy formula: 1 tablespoon general cleaning solvent, 3 tablespoons liquid dishwashing soap. Mix and apply to stain. Work in thoroughly and toss into wash. (See also p. 23)

H.P. Sauce Stain Same as *Fruit Stain, Solids*

Ink, Fountain Pen On carpets, flush with soda water. Blot. Apply shaving foam or carpet shampoo. Work in. Flush again. Blot 1 to 2 hours.

On washable fabrics, flush with cold water. Work liquid detergent in with fingers. Rinse. Repeat if necessary. Add a few drops of lemon juice or white vinegar to any remaining stain. Rinse thoroughly.

Iodine Stain On washable or unwashable fabrics, pour on more iodine, or use rubbing alcohol, and rinse with lukewarm water.

Iron Clean melted plastic off the bottom of your steam iron by setting iron at medium heat, and sprinkling a piece of brown paper with a small amount of salt. Iron the salt on the paper until the melted plastic is removed. Or, on a *cold iron,* apply a small amount of acetone with a cotton ball. Clean general dirt off irons with cleaning solvent on a soft cloth, but *only on an unplugged, cold iron.*

Ivory Never use bleach, ammonia, or solvents on genuine ivory. Clean with milk on an old toothbrush, or use toothpaste and lukewarm water. Rinse with cool water and polish with a soft cloth. Work on only a small area at a time.

Jade Wash with soap-and-water solution. Never use detergents. Buff with soft, clean, dry cloth or chamois.

Jam and Jelly Stain On carpet, scrape off excess and follow same procedure as for fruit and fruit juice stains, except use warmer water, to speed up dissolving of sugar. (See also story of mink coat, p. 18.)

Jewelry Clean jewelry with great caution. Pearls should never be washed. Your skin oils help keep them shining. Opals and turquoise should never be soaked in water. Consult your jeweler, rather than risk harming your precious, expensive items.

Ketchup Stain Same as *Fruit Stain, Solids*

Kettles To ensure inside of either electric or stove-top kettle remains scale-free, drop a glass marble inside and leave it. Minerals will adhere to marble instead of kettle. Before adding marble to old kettle, descale by soaking baking soda-and-vinegar solution inside for 24 hours. Rinse thoroughly.

Kitchen Knife Storage Use a wooden knife block and store good kitchen knives in slots blade down. This does cause blades to become dull faster, but may avoid a serious accident. Remove unidentified stains from steel blades with toothpaste and lukewarm water applied with an old toothbrush.

Kool Aid Stain On washable fabric, rinse in lukewarm water and apply a small amount of liquid detergent, worked in with fingers. Rinse in lukewarm water. If stain remains, soak in water-and-borax solution, before laundering.

On nonwashables, isolate stain, rinse carefully under cold water. Apply small amount of liquid detergent to neutralize the acid. Rinse in cool water.

On carpet, apply soda water, and blot with thick pad of clean, damp cloths. Apply shaving foam or carpet shampoo, work in, flush with soda water, and blot again. Continue blotting, wringing out pad, and replacing it until liquid has been drawn up from fibers.

Krazy Glue See *Glue*

Lampshades Check manufacturer's instructions. Some lampshades may be cleaned by immersing in warm, sudsy water. On delicate fabrics, a dry cleaner such as cornstarch, cornmeal, or commercial cleaner will remove general grease and dirt. If spots persist, use a dry solvent aerosol spray such as K2r.

Leather (Not including Suede) On greasy or oily stains, apply a dry cleaner such as cornstarch to soak up oil. Take expensive leather clothing to a good dry cleaner who specializes in leather. Keep shoes, boots, etc., looking new by cleaning once a month with saddle soap and a good leather cream. For general care of leather jackets, apply a good leather cleaner with a soft, clean cloth. On upholstery, a good leather and vinyl foam cleaner is very effective. Your local leather goods store should be able to assist you.

Light Bulbs Remove from socket when cool. Dust off with a soft, damp cloth. If excessively dirty, mix lukewarm water and dishwashing soap, and apply with a damp cloth. Be careful not to wet metal end. Dry bulb thoroughly before replacing in socket. Never clean bulbs when in the socket.

Light Fixtures, Switches, Etc. To wipe dirt and grease off plastic switches, use a damp cloth. If it's excessively dirty, use a little liquid detergent and lukewarm water. Brass switch plates and fixtures may be polished with toothpaste applied with an old brush if no commercial cleaner is available. Clean ceramic fixtures with a solution of 5 parts water to 2 parts vinegar. Add enough household cleaner to provide suds. If surface is nonporous, use liquid glass cleaner.

Linoleum Care Never use solvent. Sponge mop with nonsolvent cleaner diluted with lukewarm water for regular cleaning. For sticky jam spots, etc., scrape up with plastic or wooden spatula and wash as normal. See also *Tiles*

Lipstick See *Oil Stain, also Alcohol*

Liqueur Stain, Cream-Based Liqueurs On washable fabrics, isolate the stain, place under cool-water tap, rinse, and apply liquid detergent. On more delicate fabrics, use hand soap. Work stain between fingers and rinse continuously. If sticky residue remains, re-apply liquid detergent to which 3 or 4 drops of cleaning solvent have been added. Work in and rinse thoroughly with lukewarm water. Be sure to isolate the stain and work from the outside in to avoid spreading.

On carpet, flush with soda water and blot up as much liquid as possible. Add shaving foam or carpet shampoo, flush with soda water, and blot again. Some carpets may be treated with a mixture of 1 cup water, 2 tablespoons ammonia, and 1 tablespoon mild detergent. First test a small, unseen area before using ammonia mixture.

On nonwashable fabrics, isolate the stain, sponge up as much liquid as possible, and follow same procedure as with washable fabrics. This sticky solution of sugar, cream, and alcohol can be very difficult to lift out. It may be a job for a professional when delicate garments are involved. Judge accordingly.

Liqueur (Not Cream Based) Same as *Fruit Juice Stain*

Liquor Stain For white rings on furniture, see *Furniture*.

For liquor mixed with tomato juice, orange juice, or soft drinks, see *Fruit Juice Stain*.

Makeup Stain On washable fabrics, apply liquid detergent to which a few drops of cleaning solvent have been added. Work into fabric and rinse with lukewarm water. Repeat as necessary.

For liquid makeup on carpeting, follow same procedure as for *Oil*. For powder, vacuum immediately. Then use a soft, dry brush to brush up nap while vacuuming at the same time. Never apply moisture to powder stain unless everything else has failed.

Maple Syrup Same as *Molasses*

Margarine Same as *Fat* and *Oil*

Marmalade Same as *Jam and Jelly Stain*

Mascara See *Makeup*

Mayonnaise Same as *Oil*

Milk Stain The lower the fat content, the easier a milk stain is to remove. Sponge washable fabrics immediately with cool water, and add liquid detergent, shaving foam, or a mild liquid household cleaner. Do not use heated water, it will cook the milk solids into fabric.

For milk on fabric, treat whole milk and 2 percent the same as *Oil*. For skim milk, blot up excess, apply cool water and shaving foam, and blot again.

Molasses (Also use same procedure for *Black Bean Sauce, Coffee, Oyster Sauce, Pancake Syrup, Soy Sauce, Tea, Teriyaki Sauce, and Worcestershire Sauce Stain*) On washable fabric, flush stain with lukewarm water and sudsy ammonia, after placing an absorbent cloth behind stain to prevent transfer. Work stain from outside in. If stain is large, soak in 1 quart of lukewarm water to which 1/2 cup of borax has been added. Never use chlorine bleach.

On nonwashables, isolate stain and use lukewarm to warm water and a small amount of liquid soap. Work stain between fingers. Repeat as necessary, and blot area dry quickly. If stain persists, you may wish to try a small amount of lemon juice on area, then rinse in cool water. On valuable garments, take to dry cleaner.

On carpet, treat the same as jam or jelly stains. However, if patch spreads larger and brown tinge remains, phone your professional carpet cleaner, as residue very often remains in carpet nap and in underlay. Keep the stained area damp with lukewarm soda water solution, and keep applying the pack of wrung-out blotter cloths, tamping down with your foot and allowing to draw out liquid for up to 2 hours at a time.

Some carpets may be treated with a mixture of 1 cup water, 2 tablespoons ammonia, and 1 tablespoon mild detergent. First test a small, unseen area before using ammonia mixture.

Musk Odor For severe cases, read "Dog vs Skunk" on page 38. For small incidents, involving other animals such as cats, neutralize the odor with an acidic solution such as lemon juice or vinegar.

Mustard Stain Same as *Fruit Stain, Solids*

Nail Polish On washable fabrics, providing they are colorfast, remove nail polish carefully with an oil-free thinner or acetone. First try solvent on a small area of garment that will not be seen, to make sure it does not remove dye from fabric. On nonwashable fabrics, take to dry cleaner.

On wool and natural-fiber carpets, apply cleaning solvent or paint thinner to remove excess as quickly as possible. Blot with clean, dry cloths. In 2 separate pans, pour small amount of solvent. Use one for cleaning and the other for rinsing brush. Dip a soft bristle brush or an old toothbrush in the first pan, apply solvent to stain, brush up, and blot. Rinse brush in second pan, and repeat. Be careful to blot after each application with a clean portion of cloth, to avoid spreading stain.

Solvent may not damage carpet fiber but can soften the latex carpet backing, causing fibers to come loose. Do not pull on carpet fibers, or vacuum, until softened backing has completely dried.

On synthetic carpet fibers, nail polish removers or solvents may dissolve the carpet fibers. Test on a small area that will not be seen, or consult your carpet dealer. It may be a job best left to a professional carpet cleaner.

Neoprene Rubber *(Diving suits, windsurfing suits, wet suits, etc.)* After each use, rinse thoroughly in clean water. If possible, soak in bathtub several hours. If used in salt water, soak once a week and apply either a grease stick or graphite to metal zippers. If neoprene develops a musty odor, soak in a solution of water and household antiseptic, 2 tablespoons to each gallon of water, and rinse thoroughly in clean water. Do not use soap, as it is very difficult to rinse out.

Oil-based Paint Stain Remove from washable white and colorfast fabrics with solvent, paint thinner, or

turpentine. Apply as needed, then rinse in warm, sudsy water before laundering.

On carpet, same as *Nail Polish*

Oil Paintings Remove general dust with a very soft brush or feather duster. Never use anything hard, as you may chip and damage your work of art. For serious cleaning problems, check your Yellow Pages for someone who specializes in Art Cleaning and Restoration.

Oil Stain Sprinkle spot with cornstarch and pat in with hand. Add more if necessary to absorb oil. Brush off or vacuum up oily cornstarch. On washable fabrics, treat with liquid soap to which a few drops of cleaning solvent have been added. Work in with fingers. Rinse with lukewarm water. Repeat if necessary.

On nonwashable fabrics, place towel behind stain to prevent transfer, and apply cleaning solvent with a soft, absorbent cloth. Always work stain from outside toward center to avoid spreading. If any stain remains, have garment dry-cleaned.

Oyster Juice Same as *Egg*

Oyster Sauce Same as *Molasses*

Paint, Latex-Based On washable fabrics, flush with cold water, then wash with liquid detergent immediately—before paint sets. Once dried, the rubberized base is virtually impossible to remove without a special latex thinner. You must be extremely careful, as thinner can damage even washable fibers. It may be possible on heavier fabrics to use a fine sandpaper to remove surface stain. The secret, on all fibers including nonwashables and carpets, is to treat latex paint with soap and cool water, before it dries. In case of a large paint spill, keep the paint damp and call a professional carpet cleaner.

Perspiration Stain On washable fabrics, use sudsy ammonia and lukewarm water. Work stain directly between fingers. Fabrics exposed for long periods of time to much perspiration may be impossible to clean thoroughly. Add 1/4 to 1/2 cup of borax to regular detergent when machine washing, or use sudsy ammonia with detergent. Wash stained running shoes in machine with other wash, but be careful never to use chlorine bleach, as it can deteriorate the rubber.

On synthetic fabrics, use sudsy ammonia and lukewarm water as above. Silk and wool should be dry-cleaned only. In the case of all perspiration stains that are in washable fabrics, pre-treat with an enzyme soak before laundering.

People who are bothered by excessive perspiration may not be aware that underarm guards are available to protect garments from stains. Ask at your department store. A surgical treatment may also be possible for individuals whose perspiration is a serious problem. Ask your doctor about sweat-gland removal.

Pianos To clean exterior surface, damp mop with a vinegar-and-water solution and dry immediately. To maintain the shine, always wax with a hard furniture wax containing a high percentage of beeswax or carnauba wax. *Never clean*

or dust pianos or piano keys with a furniture dusting spray.
At least once a week, vacuum the inside of your piano
with a furniture-brush attachment, to prevent dust build-
up which can damage hammers and pads. Use the crevice
tool for the most difficult-to-reach areas.

Piano Keys Today most are made from high-quality plastic
or another synthetic material instead of ivory. To clean
and retain luster, damp mop with a solution of 1 part
vinegar to 5 parts water. For sticky and persistent stains,
damp mop keys with a cloth dampened in a mild solution
of lukewarm water and soap. Dry immediately, to avoid
moisture residue seeping into the action. This is
absolutely essential with electronic keyboards, which
should *be cleaned only after unplugging.*

Picture Frames Vacuum or dust regularly to prevent build-
up. Ornate or antique frames should be dusted only with
a soft brush. If grimy or heavily soiled, carefully wipe
with soft cloth dampened in strong (2:1) vinegar-and-
water solution. Use cotton-tipped swab for gentle
cleaning of hard-to-reach crevices.

Pillows Before cleaning, check manufacturer's instuctions
on label. A good pillow can be revitalized by tumbling it
in the dryer, without heat, for a few minutes. Soiled
pillows filled with washable material may be washed in
the washing machine. Do them one pillow per load, using
gentle cycle, washing with a little sudsy ammonia added
to the water. Send feather pillows out for a professional
cleaner to remove the feathers, clean, and re-stuff.

Plumbing Stains on metal bathroom fixtures such as taps,
soap-dishes, etc., can be removed by using toothpaste on
an old brush. For a more antiseptic approach, sudsy
ammonia and an old toothbrush will clean very
effectively. Try using your old toothbrush to clean those
hard-to-reach cracks between tiles in the shower and over
the tub. Your easily available powder cleansers do an
excellent job here. On acrylic tubs, be sure to use liquid
cleaners only, as powders may be too abrasive and could

permanently mar the surface. Another word of caution: *never mix ammonia and household bleach together,* to clean the toilet bowl or anything. It will release dangerous gases which can be explosive as well as carcinogenic. You can sanitize the inside of the toilet bowl effectively by making a slushy mix of 1 cup salt and 1½ cups vinegar to 1 cup water, if you have no commercial cleaner available. Apply with toilet-bowl brush and lots of elbow grease. On tub or sink, use same mixture with sponge, and be sure to rinse off immediately and flush with cold water to prevent salt from corroding metal parts.

Porcelain Valuable porcelain dolls, figurines, etc., should be dusted regularly or vacuumed, using brush attachment. This ceramic material is delicate and highly porous, and you should not attempt to wash it yourself. In cases of extreme yellowing or staining, consult a reputable jewelry store to see if they can clean fragile porcelain.

Powders, Spilled On Carpet Or Fabric Vacuum immediately, using crevice tool. Where powder lies on very fine fabric such as silk, place powder stain over hair dryer and turn on to air only, no heat setting, to blow powder from fibers. Never apply any liquid to a powder stain.

Powders, To Keep From Caking In high humidity areas, place a few grains of rice into the container with your baby powder or face powder. The rice will absorb moisture to keep powder dry. This also helps keep the salt in your shaker flowing freely, even when it rains. Try to keep powders stored in a tightly sealed glass jar. Remove only a small amount at a time to keep in your applicator container. It will stay fresher longer.

Red Wine Stains Back stained area of washable fabric with absorbent cloth to prevent stain from spreading to rest of garment. Flood stain with soda water. Then work liquid dishwashing detergent, white vinegar, and sudsy ammonia into stain with your fingers. Flush thoroughly with cold water.

Another method, which I don't suggest using because it wastes good wine, is to remove the red wine stains with white wine. Dry white wine, never sweet. Champagne would probably work even better. Imagine using Dom Perignon to remove the Chateau LaTour stains from your Mickey Mouse T-shirt!

On carpeting, treat red wine stains quickly. Soak up as much liquid as you can with clean cloths. Then flood area with soda water and apply blotter cloths. Wring out cloths, repeat with more soda water, and blot again. To prevent spreading, work from outside of stain inwards to center. Rinse out and wring out blotting cloths after each application. As residue fades, leave blotter pads on for increasingly longer periods. For the most stubborn stains, call a professional carpet cleaner, or rearrange the furniture!

Rubber-Backed Rugs and Bath Mats Never add bleach to the regular wash water. It will deteriorate the rubber. Dry in dryer without heat; tumble dry only with cold air.

Rugs Before cleaning stains from multicolored rugs, test them for colorfastness. Inexpensive multicolored rugs especially tend to bleed colors when cleaning solutions and even water are put on.

To prevent spreading, work from outside of stain inwards to center. Rinse and wring out blotting cloths after each application. As residue fades, leave blotter pads on for increasingly longer periods. For the most stubborn stains, call a professional carpet cleaner.

Rust Stains On whites or washable colors, dampen stain with lemon juice or a mixture of 5 parts water to 2 parts hydrogen peroxide. Allow solution to soak in up to 45 minutes. Then launder normally.

Rust stains on carpeting may be treated with a mixture of vinegar and water, lemon juice and water, or sudsy ammonia and lemon juice. Use an old toothbrush to work soluion into fibers. Finish by applying shaving or carpet-solution foam to carpet, and wipe off with damp cloth. Try to keep liquids on top of carpet as much as possible.

Scorch Marks On cottons, wools, even some silks and carpeting, lightly stroke the scorch with the finest grit sandpaper you can find, until the darkened area disappears. For severe burns, such as cigarette burns on carpet, see *Burns*.

Scratches In Wooden Furniture Rub the meat of a walnut into a scratch on walnut furniture, then buff with cloth in the direction of the grain. Treat teak wood with teak oil. Colored furniture crayons are available in shades ranging from pine to mahogany.

Shoepolish Stain Same as *Oil* or *Alcohol*

Silver Polish If commercial silver polish is not available, use toothpaste. Do not use salt and vinegar, or ketchup, on silver.

Slate Clean soot from fireplace slate by washing with sudsy ammonia and a stiff brush. Rinse thoroughly and dry immediately. When thoroughly dry, apply a hard paste floorwax to seal the porous stone and give it a shine.

Soup Stain For homemade soup stains, follow the same procedure as treating juice or vegetable stains. For very greasy soups, follow procedure for *Fat*. However, if soup is made from powder base with artificial coloring, it may be necessary for you to use a mild hydrogen-peroxide solution or sudsy ammonia along with the regular procedure to do a thorough job.

Sugar Store sugar in a tightly sealed glass or plastic container along with 1/2 cup of uncooked rice, in an old teaball or wrapped in cheesecloth. This is especially helpful for storing sugar in a boat or in your summer cottage during the winter season.

Tar Stain Same as *Creosote*

Tea Stain Same as *Coffee Stain*

Teapots Tea Grannies inform me that, unless your teapot

has become stained with something other than tea, you should never clean it with anything at all except for rinsing it with cool water. The more a teapot is used, the better the tea it will brew. For removing a foreign substance from inside, fill with lukewarm water and 1 teaspoon of baking soda before scouring.

Telephone Clean regularly with a cloth dampened in water and sudsy ammonia or liquid detergent. White telephones tend to yellow on their handle areas. To return them to their original color and luster, rub on toothpaste with an old cloth, or use old toothbrush, then wipe off.

Thawing Frozen Foods The best way, time permitting, is in the refrigerator. The longer thawed food sits out at room temperature, the greater the risk of a dangerous bacteria growth, especially in fish and poultry. A better way is to place frozen food in a plastic bag, carefully seal it, and put it into a sink filled with warm water.

Thumb Sucking May be related to a psychological disorder, or may be simply a highly conditioned habit. I do not recommend using nasty-tasting materials or wearing special gloves, or any home cure without the assistance of a trained medical or psychological practitioner. Especially if the thumb sucker is age 40 or older.

Tiles, Plastic, and Linoleum To remove general daily grunge, wash with a liquid household cleaner and a sponge mop. Avoid flooding with too much water. When cleaning linoleum, be careful cleaner does not contain solvents which may dissolve the material. Use same procedure for ceramic tiles as for plastic. On difficult stains, add sudsy ammonia to water. Use toothpaste on an old toothbrush to clean difficult stains in cracks between tiles.

Toaster Before cleaning, or before removing a stuck piece of bread, *always unplug the toaster first.* At least once a week, open the trap on the bottom and shake out the crumbs. Check the inside periodically to ensure large pieces of bread have not become jammed inside. A quick vacuuming with the crevice tool will clean the interior. Clean exterior with sudsy ammonia or liquid detergent on a damp cloth. Wipe dry before using, to avoid baking soap film onto surface. If plastic from bread wrapper melts onto hot toaster, scrape off with wooden spoon or plastic spatula while still warm. If hardened, remove with solvent on a soft cloth. Avoid using any abrasive cleaners on shiny surface.

Tools Remove rust from garden tools, hedge shears, etc., with Trisodium Phosphate and a wire brush. To prevent rust returning, apply a film of mineral oil, motor oil, or cooking oil with a clean cloth.

Toys, Plush Check manufacturer's label to see if stuffed bunnies or bears are machine washable. Many are. If not, sprinkle "fur" with cornstarch, and brush out with a good bristle brush. Brush in one direction, to remove dirty cornstarch. Vacuum out any remaining powder. For severe stains, apply shaving foam or carpet shampoo, wipe off with damp cloth, and dry with hair dryer while brushing.

Tree Sap Remove from car exterior, blue jeans, etc., with turpentine or cleaning solvent on a soft cloth. Wash with sudsy, lukewarm water, and rinse clean.

Trisodium Phosphate A highly effective, but highly corrosive cleaner, available from hardware stores. Useful for cleaning masonry and concrete. *It is very poisonous and can burn the skin.* Make sure you read the instructions thoroughly and understand them completely before using this powerful chemical.

Turmeric See *Curry*

Typewriter (White Opaque) Correcting Liquid Remove stains from washable and colorfast fabrics with solvent made by correcting liquid manufacturer, or use rubbing alcohol or acetone. On synthetics, first try solvent on a small, unseen area of garment, to make sure it will not remove color or damage fabric.

Ultraviolet Rays If you must expose your skin to the sun or to suntanning parlors, use a very effective sun screen. Leading dermatologists worldwide agree that the number of cases of skin cancer caused by exposure to ultraviolet rays is increasing. To use anything less than a number 15 sun screen product is foolhardy. As in playing Russian roulette, the choice is yours.

Urine Stain On washable and colorfast fabrics, soak quickly in cold water. Pre-soak in a borax solution or sudsy ammonia and an enzyme pre-treat before laundering. On nonwashable fabrics, isolate the stained area, flood with soda water (bottled or mix 1 tablespoon baking soda to 1 pint water), rinse with cool water, and take to dry cleaner.

On carpets, flood with soda water and blot up with thick pad of clean, dampened towels. Wring out and tamp down again with foot and allow to draw liquid from fibers. Next, apply a solution of lukewarm water, household disinfectant, and sudsy ammonia. Work stain from outside in. Soak up liquid with several more blotter applications. Flush clean with soda water, and blot again until stain is gone.

Velvet To avoid stains, new velvet upholstery should be treated with a waterproofing solution by a professional. This will save you a lot of problems later.

To treat stains, first blot up spilled liquid or carefully scrape off solids as quickly as possible. Apply soda water sparingly and blot up quickly. If stain remains, apply shaving foam but do not rub. You may damage the fabric. Allow foam to sit for a minute, then blot up with a damp, clean cloth over the area, tamp it down with your hand, and allow to sit for 30 minutes. Rinse, wring out, and reapply, to draw out stain.

Velvet, when dampened, tends to leave water rings and a flattened nap. Never back-comb damp velvet.

Do not use a home method for large stains or stains from oils, greases, or sugars. Trust your professional cleaner.

Vomit On carpet, remove solids, blot up liquid, and apply mixture of 2/3 cup water to 1/3 cup vinegar to 1 tablespoon liquid detergent. Apply pad of towels, tamped down over area, to draw up liquid.

Whipped Cream Stain Same as *Fat*

Whipping Cream, How-To Place beaters and bowl in freezer 15 minutes prior to whipping. Do not add sugar to cream until it begins to stiffen, then add gradually.

Yellowed Fabrics Avoid by storing with plenty of air circulation. Wrap in blue tissue paper, not in plastic. To whiten yellowed washable fabrics, soak in a solution of 6 parts water to 1 part hydrogen peroxide for 2 to 3 hours. For more minor yellowing, decrease strength to 8:1. Borax powder may be substituted for hydrogen peroxide. Mix 1/4 cup of borax to a gallon of water for a pre-soak. Launder as usual. Do not use chlorine bleach. Excessive yellowing of white fabrics may be caused by using too much soap and chlorine bleach.

Yolk See *Egg Stain*

Zinc Oxide Stain Same as *Fat* and *Oil Stain*

Metric Conversions

Conversions are approximate. Recommended: purchase metric measuring units.

Liquid measure

1 fl. oz.	=	30 mL
1 pint (20 fl. oz)	=	500 mL
1 cup (8 US fl. oz)	=	250 mL
1 tablespoon	=	15 mL
1 teaspoon	=	5 mL

Oven Temperature Rule of thumb = Oven temperatures in Celcius are approximately ½ those in Fahrenheit; reduce by 10°C for ovenproof glassware.

To convert minutes per pound to minutes per killogram, double the time and add 10 percent.

For gas oven settings, consult manufacturer's instructions.

Weight

1 kg.	=	2.2 lb
1 lb	=	.45 kg

Rule of thumb = To convert pounds to kilograms, multiply by .45.

To convert kilograms to pounds, multiply by 2.2.

Measure

1 in	=	25.4 mm

Index

Recipes